The Angel Years

By John Isaac Jones

Table of Contents

1 1
2 18
3 34
4 44
5 56
6 74
7 84
8 97
9 115

The Angel Years

1

Now we Johnsons were just simple country folks. Like most of the other families in Hawkins Valley, Georgia, we farmed the land, went to church and school, and tried to present ourselves as God-fearing, respectable members of the community. In all, there were five of us: Mama and Daddy and us three girls. My sister Audrey was the oldest at age 19; then there was me, Cornelia, in the middle at 15, and finally, Betty Jean, the youngest at 13. Since we lived on a farm, we always had plenty to eat and decent clothes to wear, but not any of the so-called "luxuries." Daddy worked in the fields minding the cotton and corn crops, Mama cooked and kept house, and me and the other two girls helped any way we could with the vegetable garden, the chickens, milking the cows, and feeding the hogs. Although it was 1954, we didn't have a television, but we did have a telephone and indoor plumbing. We never went on vacation and we never dreamed of owning a fancy car, so we all rode around in Daddy's old Chevy pickup truck with bald tires and floppy fenders. Like I said, we were just simple country folks. We didn't have a lot of material things, but we had our pride.

***

It all started one sunny Saturday morning in late March when my youngest sister Betty Jean blurted out these four words while we were in the backyard washing clothes.

"I think I'm pregnant."

She didn't look at me when she said it; she just kind of stared straight down at the washboard where she was grating Mama's old blue print dress up and down across the ridges. I heard her words, but, since she was always funning, I wasn't sure I had heard correctly.

"What?"

She didn't answer again right away.

"I think I'm pregnant."

"Why do you say that?"

"I haven't had a period in two months."

I started shaking my head in disbelief.

"Mama is going to have a raving fit."

"Daddy's the one I'm scared of."

"Oh, he'll rave and rant and threaten, but Mama will have the final say-so. Who's the daddy?"

Betty Jean looked up from the washboard. She hesitated, then finally spoke.

"Shadrack Griffin."

The Angel Years

"The one that drives the school bus?"

"That's him."

My heart sank as I fished another pair of Daddy's denim overalls out of the wash pot and dipped them into the rinse tub to cool.

"Have you told him?"

"Yes. Yesterday, before I got off the school bus."

"And what did he say?"

"He was mad. Cussing and fuming and carrying on. He said the baby was all mine. He said he wasn't going to have nothing to do with it."

"That's all?"

Betty Jean nodded.

"That low-down dog! I should have known. I saw you and him talking at the church picnic. How'd it happen?"

Again, she hesitated before she spoke.

"Well, you know he drives the school bus and our house is the last stop on the route. Me and him stopped down at the creek a few times and started messing around. You know… one thing led to another…"

"You make it sound like it was no big deal."

"It wasn't… at the time."

I could feel the anger growing in my guts, refusing to believe my closest sister had been so careless. Finally, I blurted it out.

"Now you're pregnant!"

She turned angrily to me.

"Not so loud! We've got to keep it a secret. You

ain't going to tell Mama, are you?"

I stared at her in disbelief.

"Are you crazy? We've got to tell her. You can't hide something like this from Mama. In a few months, you're going to be bigger than a barrel. How are you going to hide something like that?"

Betty Jean's face screwed up in a frown.

"Yeah, I guess you're right. Mama's going to know sooner or later."

She stopped and looked at me.

"Will you tell her?"

"Yeah. I'll tell her. Maybe she won't be as hard on you if I tell her."

"Thanks! You ever know anybody that's been to one of those homes for unwed mothers?"

"No."

"When are you going to tell Mama?"

"Tomorrow…. after church."

***

The following day, like most Sunday mornings, we put on our church clothes and attended services at the Old Harmony Baptist Church over at Morgan's Crossroads. On Sundays, Mama would always start the afternoon meal in the morning before we left for church. That way, by the time the sermon finished at noon and we got home, she could finish quickly so we could all eat by about 1 p.m. During those times, my mother, a smallish, leathery woman in her early forties, was a blur of constant motion in the kitchen. One moment, she would be stirring the green beans; seconds later, she would be turning the frying chicken, then putting more wood in the cook stove, then checking the biscuits, then throwing the tea bags into the boiling water. While she was darting about, I went into the kitchen and took a seat at the table.

"Mama!"

She was stirring the green beans when she glanced up at me.

"Yes, Cornpone."

Mama always called me "Cornpone." Somehow, she got that out of Cornelia. Cornpone is corn bread made without milk or eggs and is usually baked or fried. I loved to eat it, but I didn't particularly like it as a nickname. It sounded so plain and homely, but I never said anything. After all, she was my mama.

"I have something to tell you."

"It better be important. I'm busy."

She stopped briefly, then reached both hands behind her head and, for a moment, fidgeted with the bun of salt and pepper hair at the nape of her neck. Then, almost absently, she returned her attention to me.

"What do you want to tell me?"

"I hope you won't be too mad…"

"Are you in trouble at school?"

"No!"

"Then say what you got to say! I'm busy."

I waited still another moment, then blurted it out.

"Betty Jean is going to have a baby."

As I said it, she was reaching into the oven to remove a pan of hot biscuits. Seconds later, as she placed the pan on top of the stove, the thought registered and she instantly froze in place.

For a long moment, she peered at me.

"What did you say?"

"Betty Jean is going to have a baby."

"Lord God! Where did you hear that?"

"She told me. She hasn't had a period in over two months."

Mama continued to stare at me as if she were collecting her thoughts. Finally, she spoke.

"Well, I'm just going to have to talk to her. Have you told anybody else?"

"No."

"Well, don't mention it to anybody else in the family until I can talk to her."

***

Now my mama was not the kind of person that would fly off the handle. That was Daddy's department. Mama would study something over and over before she would do anything. I knew she would talk to Betty Jean before she mentioned anything to Daddy, so I waited. That afternoon, after we had eaten and she had cleaned up the kitchen, Mama came to my and Betty Jean's room. Betty Jean and I had had our own room for as long as I could remember. Early on, Mama recognized how close we were, so she put us in the same room together. When Mama came into our room that day, she said she wanted to talk to Betty Jean in private and asked me to leave and close the door. I did as she instructed and waited outside while they talked. They were in there for over an hour. I could hear Betty Jean crying and Mama talking very sternly to her. Finally, Mama came out. Her face was red with anger and I could see she had been crying. Only moments after Mama left, I ducked back inside the bedroom.

"What did Mama say?"

"She said we needed to be sure I was pregnant first. She said she didn't want to go off half-cocked. She said she would do a test."

"A test? What kind of test?"

"Mama said she knew how to do a pregnancy test."

"How's she going to do that?"

"Not sure."

"Come on, let's go ask her."

Moments later, we were in the kitchen, where we found Mama washing the big iron skillet she used for frying chicken.

"Mama," I started. "Betty Jean said you were going to do a test to see if she was pregnant."

"I sure am," Mama said. "You girls want to watch? You might have to use it yourself one of these days."

"Does it work?"

"It worked for all three of you girls."

"When are you going to do it?"

"Soon as I finish these dishes."

She stopped.

"Do you think we should wait for Audrey?" I asked.

"She won't be here until dinner time," Mama said. Audrey had gone home from church with the Thompsons and promised to be home by dark. "I don't want to wait that long. I want to get it over and done with."

"Have you told her?" Betty Jean asked.

"No," Mama said. "She'll hear about it tonight."

***

Fifteen minutes later, Betty Jean, Mama, and I were in the old wood shed behind the house where Mama would grow tomato seedlings. On the work bench in front of her, she had a small jar containing a little bit of Betty Jean's pee, a box of baking soda, and a bowl of sugar.

"When a woman gets pregnant, nature puts a whole new set of chemicals in her body," Mama said. "If those new chemicals are in Betty Jean's body, this test will tell us."

Betty Jean and I were all eyes as we watched Mama take two level tablespoonfuls of sugar and dump them into the jar of urine. Then she opened the box of baking soda and took a pinch.

The Angel Years

"Now if the sugar doesn't dissolve when I drop in this little bit of soda, it means she's pregnant. If it dissolves, then she's not. Y'all got that?"

"Yes, Mama," we said in unison.

"Okay. Here goes!"

Both of us watched closely as Mama sprinkled the baking soda into the jar of urine. Slowly, the grains of sugar floated aimlessly down through the yellow liquid and, grain by grain, settled on the bottom of the container.

"The sugar is not dissolving," Mama said conclusively.

She turned to Betty jean.

"You're with child. That's for sure. When was the last day of your last period?"

Betty Jean reflected for a moment.

"January 18th or 19th," Betty Jean said.

Mama took a pencil out of her apron pocket and started doing calculations on the back of an empty seed packet.

"You're going to have that baby on September 8," Mama said.

***

That night, when we gathered around the table for the evening meal, Daddy hadn't come in yet. All that afternoon, he had been in the river bottoms repairing a fence. When he finally came in, he said he wanted to wash up before he ate and asked us to wait for him. Once seated, he had on a clean shirt and pants. My daddy was a big bear of a man who wore glasses and always had a stubble of beard except on Sundays. His face was sunburned and, when he took off his hat, you could see the tan line across the middle of his white forehead.

"All right, Ila," he said. "You say the blessing."

With that, Mama blessed the food and we began to eat. Over the next thirty to forty minutes, we chowed down on Mama's roast ham, green beans, and mashed potatoes and biscuits and finished up with a slab of peach cobbler. Once she was finished, Audrey got up to leave the table.

"Keep your seat, Audrey!" Mama said. "As soon as everybody is finished, we're going to have a family meeting."

"What's the meeting about?" Daddy asked.

"Go ahead and finish your meal," Mama said. "You'll find out soon enough."

Thirty minutes later, everybody had finished eating and Mama had cleared off the table. Then she took the floor.

"Now the five of us have always been a family and done everything together and it's going to stay that way. We're having this meeting because we have to decide what to do about Betty Jean's condition."

"Condition?" Daddy said. "What condition?"

"Betty Jean has got herself pregnant," Mama said.

For a moment, you could have heard a pin drop as

The Angel Years

we all waited for the thought to register with Daddy.

Slowly, Daddy turned and peered across the table at Betty Jean.

"Betty Jean?" he said. "Is that right?"

"Yes, Daddy."

"Who's the daddy?"

"Shadrack Griffin."

"That brown-haired kid that drives the school bus?"

Betty Jean nodded.

"Are y'all going to get married?"

"No, Daddy."

Daddy inhaled and looked away.

"Have you told him?"

"Yeah. I told him last Friday when I got off the school bus."

"And what did he say?"

"He said he didn't have time to raise a child."

Daddy's face screwed up in anger. For a long moment, he didn't speak.

"That low-down rascal," he said finally. "He's going to do right by you. I'm going to see to that. Tomorrow I'm going to get my shotgun and go down and have a talk with him."

Mama could see that Daddy was becoming agitated.

"Horace!!! Calm down!!" Mama said. "That's why I didn't tell you. You're always so cock-sure about these things."

"This is our daughter we're talking about here," Daddy said, pointing to Betty Jean. "I'm not going to let some no-count do this to my daughter."

"Can you be reasonable for once in your life?" Mama said.

"So what do you want to do?"

"We're both going to talk to him tomorrow and see if he'll do the right thing."

"Talk! Talk! Talk! In these situations, you can't talk people into doing something. You have to make them do it. Tomorrow I'm going to get my shotgun and go make him do the right thing by my daughter."

"No!" Mama said again. "You ain't going to do no such thing. We're both going to talk to him. If we can't convince him, there's not going to be any violence."

Daddy glowered at Mama for a long moment.

"Now listen here, Ila…"

Mama turned to face him.

"No! You listen, Horace! You always feel like you can make other people do what you want. You think all you got to do is show somebody a gun and they'll do what you say. That's the way it used to be. It ain't like that anymore."

"I can scare hell out of him."

"All you'll do is make him mad."

"No, I'm going to tell him if he can't do the right thing by my girl, I'm going to kill him."

"Then where will that leave us?" Mama said. "You'll be in prison and me and these girls will be without a father and a husband. No, tomorrow we'll go talk to him together."

The Angel Years

"I'm taking my shotgun!"

"No!" Mama said. "You ain't taking no shotgun."

***

Late that afternoon, as usual, Audrey, Betty Jean, and I headed to the barn to milk the cows. We had two cows, Topsy and Flossie; I would milk one and Audrey would milk the other. With each cow, me and Audrey milked the two big front teats for the table and saved the smaller back teats for the calves. Betty Jean's job was to tussle the two calves in and out of the stalls to the cows so they could suckle, then get them back into the stall when they were finished.

As we walked, Audrey kept glancing over at Betty Jean. I knew she was going to start trouble. Since she was the oldest, she thought it was her job to boss me and Betty Jean around. At age 19, she was the biggest of us three girls. Tall for her age, Audrey had a pleasant face, long brown hair, and wore thick glasses. When Audrey was born, doctors said she would have to wear glasses until she got a special eye operation. The operation cost way more money than Mama and Daddy had, so Audrey had been wearing glasses all of her life.

Finally, Betty Jean looked back at her.

That was all the opening Audrey needed.

"Don't you have a lick of sense?" Audrey started. "What you doing letting that no-good Shadrack Griffin go playing with yo' tomato. You're not even fourteen years old. Now your life is going to be ruined."

Betty Jean didn't reply. She glanced over at me for help.

Audrey stopped.

"Did you hear me?" she shouted at Betty Jean. "I'm talking to you."

"You shut up!" Betty Jean shot back. "You don't run my life!!"

"No, you shut up!" Audrey said. "Somebody's going to have to knock some sense into that thick head of yours."

Then, in a sudden flash of anger, Audrey turned, grabbed Betty Jean by the shoulders, and started shaking her. Betty Jean tried to fend of the attack as best she could, but Audrey was much stronger and bigger.

"Stop!! Stop!" Betty Jean screamed, slapping frantically at Audrey with both hands. As Betty Jean tried to pull away, Audrey grabbed her hair so she couldn't escape.

"Turn her loose," I shouted.

As if she had not heard, Audrey angrily jerked Betty Jean's hair harder as the younger sister yelled in pain. I stepped forward and slapped Audrey hard across the face. The pain of the blow startled her and she released Betty Jean's hair. Then she came at me, fists first. Although I was four years younger, I was almost as big and strong as she was. When she grabbed me in a bear hug, I wrestled her to the ground and we rolled over and over in the grass. Suddenly, Audrey's glasses fell off

The Angel Years

and she stopped fighting.

"Wait! Wait!" she shouted. "I've lost my glasses."

I stood up and looked down at her.

"My glasses!! My glasses! Where are my glasses?"

Helplessly, she floundered about the ground, feeling in the grass for her glasses. She was blind without them. I walked over and retrieved her glasses.

"I've got your glasses," I said.

"Give 'em to me!!" she said. "I can't see without them."

"Only if you'll promise to leave Betty Jean alone."

"Give me my glasses!" Audrey shouted.

"No!" I said again. "I'll give you the glasses only if you'll promise…"

I waited.

"Okay!" Audrey said finally. "I promise."

I handed her the glasses. She put them on.

For a moment, still sitting on the ground, she looked up at me, then to Betty Jean. She was still angry, but the fight was gone. Finally, her eyes stopped on Betty Jean.

"I can't believe you would do something like this to yourself," she said. "You better be glad you're not a daughter of mine. I'd whip your butt all the way from here to Albany."

"That's enough!" I said. "Come on!! Let's get these cows milked."

***

The following morning, which was Monday, there was a new driver on the school bus, a fat, round-faced woman named Tina Mae. I knew that didn't look good for Betty Jean, but I didn't say anything. All that day at school, I wondered what happened when Mama and Daddy went to talk to Shadrack. Finally, that afternoon when me and Betty Jean got home, we rushed into the house and went straight to Mama. She was sewing up the shoulder on one of Daddy's old denim shirts.

"Did you and Daddy talk to Shadrack?" Betty Jean asked.

"There wasn't no talking to it," Mama said, piercing the garment with the needle and pulling the long thread through to make a stitch. "He flew the coop. First, we went to the saw mill. The straw boss said Shadrack told him on Saturday morning he was quitting the job and wouldn't be coming back. Then we went to his grandmother's house."

"And what did she say?" Betty jean said.

"She said he had left Saturday afternoon to go back to Kentucky. You might as well forget about him."

"I figured something like that," Betty Jean said finally. "There was a new driver on the school bus today."

Another long pause.

"It's going to be all right," Mama said, using a pair of a scissors to cut the thread. "We're going to have to deal with this baby on our own. We'll figure it out."

"What are we going to do?"

"We're going to have another family meeting tonight," Mama said, holding up the shirt to inspect her work. "We'll make a decision."

2

That night, after all of the supper dishes were washed and the table was cleared off, Mama took the floor. After she explained that Shadrack had disappeared, Mama said we were going to have to make a decision about Betty Jean's "condition."

"Looks like we're back to square one," Mama said. "Now I'm not going to have my daughter shamed like that Anderson girl over at the Crossroads. When she had a child out of wedlock, they kicked her out of church. She was the daughter of a deacon and everybody in this valley knew about it and talked about it. I know the way people are. People will see Betty Jean with that baby and they'll whisper, 'Horace Johnson's daughter has been fornicating.' I'm not going to let that happen to my daughter."

Mama looked at Daddy.

"What do you think we should do, Horace?"

"I say we send her to the doctor down in Valdosta."

"You mean you want Betty Jean to have an

abortion?"

"Yeah, that's what I'm saying. We don't need to be taking on another mouth to feed. At the rate we're going, we're never going to pay off this farm."

Mama looked at Audrey.

"What do you say, Audrey?"

"I agree," she said. "If Betty Jean already has the baby, it's going to ruin her chances of ever being married. No man wants to marry a woman with another man's child."

"Cornelia?"

"It's not right to kill an innocent little baby that's never been born," I said. "There are not enough reasons in all the world that makes it right."

"Let's be practical," Daddy said. "We don't need another mouth to feed."

For a moment, Mama looked thoughtfully at Daddy, then she turned to Betty Jean.

"What do you want to do?"

Betty Jean didn't answer at first.

"I would feel like a murderer if I killed this baby," she said finally. "I want to keep it."

"Do you realize how much time and effort and money goes into raising a child?" Daddy said.

"No amount of money or time or effort is more valuable than a human life," I said.

Another long silence.

"I'm ashamed of you," Daddy said finally, looking at Betty Jean. "We never had nothing like this in my family."

"Now don't be too hasty," Mama said. "Remember your sister Maisy…"

Daddy's head dropped.

"What happened, Mama?" I asked.

"Several years ago, your Aunt Maisy got pregnant with a no-count and they sent her to the doctor in Valdosta for an abortion. After the operation, she started flooding and almost bled to death. Your grandmother and Maisy's oldest sister kept her packed for three days. She was lucky to come out alive."

"That was a long time ago," Daddy said.

"Maybe it was," Mama said. "But something like that could happen to Betty Jean."

Another long silence.

"We're going to put it to a vote," Mama said. "The vote will decide what we're going to do. What do you say, Horace?"

"I say send her to the doctor in Valdosta. We don't need another mouth to feed."

"Audrey?"

"I agree with Daddy. No thirteen-year-old girl needs a baby that doesn't have a father."

"Cornelia?"

"I couldn't bear to take responsibility for killing an innocent little baby. If there is a God in heaven, he wouldn't agree to killing a baby. It's just not right."

Mama looked at Betty Jean.

"Betty Jean?"

The Angel Years

"I want to have this baby," she said.

"No man will ever want you," Audrey said. "You'll spend your whole life alone with that child."

"Let me be the one to worry about that. It's my baby."

"You're too young to know what you're getting into," Audrey said.

A long silence.

"How do you vote, Mama?" I asked finally.

Mama inhaled, then spoke.

"We're not going to throw this baby away like an old shoe. Betty Jean is going to have this baby and we're going to keep it a secret from the outside world."

"How we going to do that?" Audrey asked.

"I'll think of something," Mama said.

"Mama, you get some crazy ideas," Audrey said, "but this one takes the cake. You don't realize what you're doing by letting Betty Jean keep this baby."

"You shut up!!" Mama said. "We took a vote and we're going to stick by it."

"You stupid old woman!" Audrey said. "You're going to ruin Betty Jean's life."

Audrey got up to leave the table. As she stood up, Mama grabbed her arm and pushed her down into the chair.

"You keep your seat, young lady," Mama said. "I'm running this meeting. Not you!"

Audrey's face turned red with anger.

Mama glared at her.

"One of these days, I'm going to knock some sense into that thick head of yours."

Hot, angry tears welled in Audrey's eyes.

"Y'all can stop now," Daddy said. "That's enough!"

Suddenly, everybody grew quiet. Then Mama continued.

"All right. We've made our decision. Betty Jean is going to have this child and we're going to hide this pregnancy from the outside world. When she starts getting really big, I'm going to take her to the unwed mothers home in Milledgeville. If we all work together, we can do this."

She looked around the table.

"Are we agreed?"

Daddy nodded. Betty Jean and I indicated our agreement.

"Audrey?"

"You're making a big mistake by saddling Betty Jean with this baby. You'll regret it someday."

"The decision has been made," Mama said. "If you don't like the decision, you can get your things and leave this house. Do you understand?"

Audrey dropped her head in angry silence. She knew better than to argue when Mama had that tone.

"We're all going to pitch in and help Betty Jean through this. We're a family here and everybody is going to do their part. We know what we've got to do and we can do it if we all work together. All we got to do is just do it!!"

The Angel Years

She stopped and looked around the table.

"Now remember, there is nobody going to know about this except the five of us. Y'all can't tell nobody... Your friends, your uncles, your teachers... Nobody! This is our family secret."

***

So, in late March of 1954, we began our great adventure into hiding Betty Jean's pregnancy. Over the first few weeks, she didn't need much help. She showed no visible signs of pregnancy; she helped us with the chores and continued as an eighth grader at Hawkins Valley High. By late April, however, she was four months gone and we could see signs. There was a noticeable bump on her belly and she started getting really picky about what she ate. She started throwing up in the mornings and she seemed to be tired all the time. In her face, I could see the discomfort in everything she did. Then, one day when we were feeding the cows, Mama noticed that it took all the strength Betty Jean had to lift the five-gallon bucket of feed up to the trough. She called me and Audrey aside.

"Now you girls are going to give Betty Jean some relief from her chores. She's in her fifth month and she's slowing down."

And we did. When the three of us went to milk the cows, Audrey and I would tell her to just rest on the extra milking stool and we would tussle with calves. She agreed and welcomed our help.

***

The following week, Betty Jean got sick at school and called Mama and Daddy to come get her. I always hated when my parents came to the school. Mama had enough pride to dress up a little, but Daddy wore the same clothes: overalls, khaki shirt, heavy shoes, and his old brown jumper that he wore in the fields. I knew the other kids were looking at him and had him pegged as just another local farmer with calloused hands and faded overalls. I was so ashamed of my father during those times. Anyway, when Mama and Daddy arrived, the principal got me out of history class for a meeting. The principal was a small, unsmiling, gray-haired woman named Miss Strickland.

"Why was Betty Jean throwing up in the girls' room?"

"The doctor said she has got a 'nervous stomach' condition," Mama lied. "If she eats the wrong thing, it comes right back up. I'm going to have to take her out of school for a while."

"We can have the school nurse examine her."

"Oh, no!" Mama said. "That won't be necessary. Her problem has already been diagnosed. I've got medicine. I know what to do for her."

"As you wish," Miss Strickland said. "You're her mother. What about her homework assignments?"

The Angel Years

"Can Cornelia get her assignments and bring them home so Betty Jean can do them? Once they're finished, Cornelia will return them to the teachers."

Miss Strickland looked at me.

"Is that all right with you, Cornelia?"

"Yes, ma'am. That's fine."

Miss Strickland peered at Mama thoughtfully.

"That should work," she said finally. "There are only two more weeks left in the term. We can do that, but I expect the assignments to be handed in in a timely fashion."

"I promise you that the assignments will be on time."

"That will be acceptable."

***

So Betty Jean was removed from public view at the school. A month later, on a Sunday in late June, Mama made another decision. While Betty Jean was getting ready for church, Mama came to our room. When Mama walked in and saw her trying to dress herself, Mama started shaking her head.

"You're too big to go to church. If those old women get a look at you, they're going to know for sure you're with child and their tongues will be wagging. I want you to stay at home today."

So Betty Jean stayed home that Sunday and the rest of us went to Sunday services. As we started to Daddy's pickup, Mama made another announcement.

"After today, we going to quit going to church until Betty Jean has this baby."

"Why?" Daddy asked.

"There are too many nosy old women. I don't want them to start gossiping and shaming my daughter."

"If we do that," Audrey replied, "I won't get to see May Nell."

May Nell Thompson was her long-time friend from high school who she frequently visited after church.

"May Nell will have to wait," Mama said. "Betty Jean comes first."

***

As usual, when the sermon was over that Sunday, the pastor, Rev. Mize, was at the church steps saying good-bye to members. As always, Mama was up front when our family left the church.

"Mrs. Johnson!" Rev. Mize said. "I'm so happy you and your family could be with us today."

"Well, we ain't coming back until you get rid of that smell."

The reverend was taken aback at Mama's comment.

"Smell? What smell?"

"Something has gone in this church house and died. A rat, a snake, or something…. And it's stinking to high heaven. Me and my family won't be back until you get rid of that smell."

The Angel Years

"Mrs. Johnson, nobody else has smelled it."

"Well, I can!" Mama said "And we ain't coming back until you get rid of it."

"I'm very sorry," he said, "but…"

"That's all I got to say," Mama said.

Then she quickly turned and stalked down the church house steps. Without looking at the preacher, the rest of us strode down the steps behind her. Then, as the reverend watched helplessly, we headed across the churchyard to Daddy's old pickup.

***

That afternoon, like I did most Sunday afternoons, I ventured down to the catfish pond to paint pictures of birds. About fifty yards behind the barn, Daddy had a pond, maybe two acres in area, where he raised catfish. If Mama wanted a mess of fish for the table, he would wade into the pond with a net, scoop up several pounds of fresh catfish, and deliver them to Mama. Two sides of the pond were surrounded by trees and the third side by cow pasture, but a huge forest of bulrushes lived on the fourth side. I liked to sit in a grassy spot in front of the bulrushes, so I would paint the birds as they flitted about the dark green reedy plants in search of insects. Usually, when I was painting, I would spread an old quilt in front of the bulrushes and set up my easel.

That same afternoon, as usual, I saw Betty Jean, her motorcycle magazines in hand, coming down the path behind the barn to join me. At the pond, she could get away from Mama to read her "dirty magazines," as Mama called them, and smoke cigarettes. She knew Mama would have a fit if she caught her doing either one, so she would sneak around behind Mama's back. She knew I wouldn't say anything.

When she arrived, Betty Jean peered at the hummingbird I was painting.

"Oh, Cornelia," she said, taking a seat on the old quilt. "I love that. It looks so real!!"

"Thanks!"

For several minutes, she watched as I painted in a flourish of red on the hummingbird's throat. Finally, she spoke.

"Why do you spend so much time painting birds?"

"I love birds," I replied. "When you look at birds, you are looking at God's little miracles."

She studied me for a moment.

"You don't get any money for it," she said. "Why waste the time?"

"That's all right. Maybe I will get some money for them someday. If I don't, then I've had lots of fun admiring God's little creations."

Betty Jean shook her head doubtfully and opened one of the magazines. The cover read "Motorcycle Mamas."

We were quiet for several minutes while I painted and Betty Jean read her magazine. Finally, she looked up at me.

The Angel Years

"How much do you think a motorcycle would cost?"

"I don't know. I never priced one."

"If you were guessing, how much do you think one would cost?"

"I have no idea."

She returned to the magazine for a long moment then turned back to me.

"What about a tattoo? How much you think a tattoo would cost?"

I stopped painting and peered at her.

"You thinking about getting a tattoo?"

"Maybe. What's wrong with that?"

"Daddy would have a raving fit if he saw you with a tattoo."

She didn't answer at first.

"I'm not sure I care…" she said finally.

Another long silence as she buried her head in the motorcycle magazine again.

I knew Betty Jean had some wild ideas, but I thought I always felt like I knew what she was capable of doing. When she said things like that, I wasn't so sure.

"Can you imagine spending your life riding through the world on a motorcycle?" she said almost wistfully. "Just cruising along in bright sunshine, the wind in your hair, the sound of the engine below you and not a worry in the world? I don't know why people feel like they have to settle down and do the same things over and over day after day after day. The world is too big to stay cooped up all your life."

"What kind of life are you looking for?"

"I want to be free. Free from worry and work and responsibility. When I wake up every morning, the only thing I want to do is exactly what my little heart desires."

"What about money? You're going to have to work to get money to pay your bills."

"Nah! I'd find some way to make money. Do you see how Daddy worries about money all the time? I never want to be like that."

She was quiet for a moment.

"I'll never spend my life on a farm," she continued. "One of these days, I'm leaving here and never coming back."

"What about that baby you're carrying?"

She looked at me.

"I don't know. I guess I could just carry it with me."

"A child needs a place to call home. You can't expect a little baby to sleep on the side of the road every night."

She inhaled.

"Yeah, I guess you're right. I never thought of that."

***

Over the next few weeks, Betty Jean started getting big, really big. Her belly was pooched out like a knot on a log. Since she was so short and tiny anyway, the bulge at her belly stood out more than ever. As she got bigger

The Angel Years

and bigger, Mama would let out her clothes, especially her pants. Mama got the idea to sew some elastic into the waist of her pants so they would stretch and, as Mama put it: "It will make it easier on the baby."

One Saturday morning in early July, all of us went to Albany so Audrey could go to the eye doctor. Mama and Daddy were in the front seat of Daddy's pickup and we three girls were in the back. Once we arrived at the eye doctor's office, there were no parking spaces left, so Daddy parked at the Magic Burger next door. Once parked, Audrey got out and went inside while we waited in the parking lot. The Magic Burger was a drive-in that served hamburgers, fries, shakes, and such. On Saturdays, there was always a bunch of boys from Hawkins Valley High hanging out in the parking lot talking about cars, girls, and football.

Once Daddy's truck was parked, several of the boys glanced over at us. Mama had given Betty Jean one of her old long raincoats to cover her belly. There were several older boys in the crowd that Betty Jean and I knew from school. They included Ron Holloway, Wendell Jenkins, and Tommy McCartney.

Ron peered at Betty Jean.

"Oh, Betty Jean Johnson," he said. "You're such a pretty little thing. What you doing wearing that big coat? It's May."

Betty Jean looked at me.

"You hush up, Ron," I said. "Go mind your own business."

"Now, Cornelia," he replied. "You don't have to get upset. I was just bragging on your sister. We all know how pretty she is."

"Ain't that the truth," Wendell Jenkins said. "You ought to be showing off what she's got rather than hiding it."

The boys had a big laugh.

"I told y'all to shut up and leave Betty Jean alone," I said.

Another round of giggles.

Mama was sitting in the passenger seat in the front and could hear every word.

"You didn't tell us why you're wearing that coat," Tommy McCartney said. "You ain't getting fat, are you?"

"No! You blabbermouth!" I said. "She's not getting fat!"

"You ain't pregnant, are you?" said Tommy.

This brought an even bigger laugh.

I knew that would bring Mama into the conversation.

"Now you boys quit aggravating Betty Jean," she said. "Y'all leave her alone or I'll call the county on you."

The three boys drew back at Mama's words. They were quiet for a moment.

"We was just having some fun," Ron said. "We didn't mean no harm."

"Betty Jean is not laughing," Mama said.

The Angel Years

Ron turned to the other boys.

"Come on, let's go get a hamburger!"

Instantly, they turned and headed for the order window. Thirty minutes later, Audrey had finished with the eye doctor.

On the return trip, Mama was quiet for a long time. Finally, she turned to Daddy.

"Did you hear what that McCartney boy said?"

"About her being pregnant?"

Mama nodded.

"I heard what he said, but it don't mean nothing. He was just funning like boys do. He don't have a clue that Betty Jean is really pregnant."

"You don't think he suspects anything?"

"No. Nothing at all."

3

That night, after supper, Mama made a new announcement.

"It's time to send Betty Jean to Milledgeville," she said. "She's getting so big now that it's really hard to hide it. We've had good luck so far keeping this a secret and I don't want to push our luck. I'm going to take her to Milledgeville tomorrow."

"Can you give me just a little more time at home?" Betty Jean said. "I don't know those people at the home. It's going to be lonesome."

"No, I think it's time," Mama said. "That baby that's growing inside you is going to need some things we can't give it. They've got doctors and nurses and tests and such at the home. Professional medical people that can attend to yours and the baby's needs."

***

Late that night, I got out of bed and went into the

The Angel Years

kitchen to get a glass of milk. Mama and Daddy, dressed in their nightclothes, were seated at the table.

"We're going to need $85 to get Betty Jean registered at the home," Mama said.

Daddy inhaled.

"I can take some money out of savings," he said. "I hope Betty Jean's baby don't send us to the poorhouse."

"You quit talking like that," Mama said. "This is something we have to do and money hasn't got nothing to do with it. This child is going to be your flesh and blood as much as it is mine."

Daddy didn't reply.

"At the rate we're going, we're never going to pay off this farm."

"Just keep quiet and get the money."

***

The next morning, me, Audrey, Betty Jean, and Mama walked from the house to the highway so Mama and Betty Jean could catch the Greyhound bus that would take her to Milledgeville. Mama was all decked out in the dark blue dress she wore for funerals and her grey pillbox hat with the two red roses on top. Betty Jean was pretty as a picture in her pregnancy. Mama had done up her blonde hair in braids and she was wearing a pair of special light blue pants Mama had made with elastic in the waist. I hugged and kissed both of them as they boarded the bus. Audrey waved good-bye as the bus pulled away. Late that night, Mama arrived back at home. She said Betty Jean had been registered; everybody was nice to her and she was happy that Betty Jean had professional doctors now. She said the director promised that all information about Betty Jean's pregnancy would remain strictly confidential.

***

Over the next few months, we got three letters from Betty Jean. Mama asked her to write because phone calls were so expensive.

July 21, 1954
Dear Family,
I'm so glad Mama made me come early. The doctors did several tests and found that there was blockage in my right breast. They fixed it and said if they hadn't discovered it, the baby would not have gotten any milk from my right breast.

Other than that, they say I'm going to have a healthy pregnancy and should deliver on September 9. That's one day later than Mama said. You got to give Mama credit, she does pretty good without all of the scientific stuff.

They're all very nice here. My room is clean and the food is good. I'm meeting girls who are in the same situation as myself. After talking to them, I don't feel as bad about what happened.

I'll just be glad when it's over.
Betty Jean

The Angel Years

***

August 13, 1954
Dear Family,
Oh, Lord, I'll be so glad when this is over. Every move I make, every breath I take has got some connection with this baby. My back and shoulders ache from carrying this baby. My legs go weak for no reason and I spend a lot of time sitting down.

Carrying this baby is like having a little sack of cow feed tied to my middle. Anything I do, I have to consider the sack of cow feed. I have to sleep on my back night every night and it really is tiresome. When I go to sleep, I'm looking at the ceiling, and when I wake up, I'm still looking at the ceiling.

Mama was right when she said a first pregnancy changes everything about a woman. Now I can feel every part of me going through changes. I guess all I can do is let nature take its course.

I'll be so glad when this is over.
Betty Jean

***

September 6, 1954.
Dear Family,
Doctors say I will deliver any day now. All I am now is just a big blob of flesh with a little human growing inside me. I can't stand to look at myself anymore. I asked one of the girls here who just delivered if it hurts to have a baby.

She told me I have never felt the kind of pain that's involved in having a child. She said they can give you shots, but it still hurts. I guess I won't know till it happens.

It just a matter of waiting now. Lord, I'll be so glad when it's over.

Betty Jean

***

On the evening of September 8, 1954, the administrator at the Margaret Baker Home for Unwed Mothers called Mama and announced that Betty Jean had delivered a healthy eight-pound, nine-ounce baby girl and was ready to go home. Mama told the administrator she would be there the afternoon of the following day.

I will always remember the day Mama and Betty Jean came home with the baby. Daddy, Audrey, and I were all waiting at the highway to see them get off the bus. When Mama pulled back the blanket and I saw the baby's face, I was instantly in love. She was a beautiful child with a big patch of blonde hair, blue eyes, and a sort of sly half-smile. The very first time I reached down to touch her hand, she grabbed my finger and held on for dear life. At that very moment, I knew she was a special child. A very special child.

Even Daddy was happy to see the new baby. When Mama pulled back the blanket, he broke into a big smile and said: "Got eyes like her mama." Audrey, when she saw the baby, hardly broke a smile. I knew she didn't approve. She didn't approve of anything. As we walked

The Angel Years

back to the house, Audrey lagged behind, sulking like an old dog that had just been whipped. I didn't understand why anyone couldn't find joy and love in their heart for a new baby.

Once we got to the house, I knew Mama would be ready for a family meeting, so we all gathered around the table. Once everybody was seated, Mama, holding Betty Jean's baby in her arms, took the floor.

"What I'm holding here is the newest member of the Johnson family. As far as the outside world is concerned, me and your daddy are going to be this child's parents and you girls are going to have another sister."

"What are we going to call her?" I asked.

"Her name will be Shirley Temple Johnson and we're going to call her Shirley."

"Where did that come from?" Daddy asked.

Mama inhaled and looked around the table.

"If anybody wants to know where we got her, we adopted her from a Catholic Mission in California. We're going to tell the world that her natural mother, who put the baby up for adoption, was a first cousin of Shirley Temple. You know, the little girl in the movies."

"We know, Mama," Audrey said impatiently.

"That's why we're going to call her Shirley. I had some papers put together to make it look official."

She produced a newly-printed document and showed it to us.

At the top of the paper was a picture of Jesus in front

of a cross lovingly holding out his arms to a small child. The name at the top read:

Sacred Heart of Jesus Catholic Ministry, 1206 Mission Street, Los Angeles, Ca. Underneath, the text read: "On this day, Mr. and Mrs. Horace Johnson are hereby awarded the sole and final parental custody of Shirley Temple Johnson."

Also, there was another paper that read "State of California Certificate of Birth" at the top and listed the mother's name as Charlotte Ann Brown of Culver City, California and the father as "unknown." It contained all of the details of the birth.

Each of us looked at the papers.

"Mama!" Audrey said finally. "Where did you get these?"

"Never mind where they came from," Mama said. "They look official and that's all that matters. If anybody wants to see proof of our story, we have it here."

Daddy took the birth certificate and looked at it.

"Looks real," he said, handing it back to Mama. "Your mother has been talking to her sister over in Valdosta."

"Yeah, but we're not going to talk about that right now," Mama said.

Daddy was referring to Aunt Edna, Mama's sister that ran a printing company in Valdosta.

A long silence.

"Mama," Audrey said finally. "That's the biggest lie

I ever heard in my life."

Mama turned to Audrey.

"Maybe it is," Mama said. "But it's what we're going to tell the world about where this baby came from. This family has worked hard to give Betty Jean and this baby a clean start in life and we're going to keep it that way."

"What if I told…" Audrey said.

I knew that would set Mama off. Instantly, she walked around the table and handed off the baby to Betty Jean, then she went back to face Audrey. I could see the fires of hell in her eyes.

First, she got into Audrey's face and glared at her. Then, suddenly, with both hands, she grabbed the front of Audrey's dress.

"Now you hear me and you hear me good," Mama said, pulling Audrey's face to hers. "If you ever tell this, I'll hunt you down and beat the holy stuffing out of you."

Then, still grasping two fists full of Audrey's shirt, Mama waited for a reply. There was none. Audrey's face was white as a sheet. Finally, Mama released her grip. Calmer now, she turned to the other family members.

"Now, this child is going to be loved. There's not going to be any talk about how she came into this world. Nobody can change the way they were born and that's the way it's going to be with Shirley."

A pause. Then she turned back to Audrey.

"And if you don't like it, you can get up and leave this house."

Audrey didn't reply.

"Did you hear me?"

Audrey dropped her head.

"I heard."

***

Now it's safe to say that Audrey was not Mama's favorite child. In fact, it seemed that the two of them were constantly at one another's throats. Ever since I can remember, they had been fighting.

"Audrey takes after your daddy's side of the family," Mama would say when we were alone. "She's a lot like your daddy's mother... a mean, contrary woman who couldn't get along with the devil himself. What's more, having to wear glasses has done something to her head. She's thinks no man will ever love her as long as she wears glasses."

And Mama was right. Audrey would soon be twenty, but she never did anything to primp herself. She never wore lipstick or perfume or makeup and she never dressed up like she was trying to get a man. Sometimes, I would go to the door of her room and watch as she sat at the dresser looking at herself in the mirror, first with her glasses, then without them. Once, as I was watching her, she smiled when she looked at herself without glasses; then, when she returned to her glasses, she

The Angel Years

peered at herself for a long moment. Then, suddenly, she put her head on the dresser and started sobbing.

***

Over the next few weeks, everything returned to normal. Betty Jean went back to school. We started going back to church again; Betty Jean started helping with chores again and we girls had a new baby sister. It was funny how the different family members took to Shirley over the next few months. Of course, Mama and I were always there to help Betty Jean and the baby any way we could. We loved to change her diapers and powder her bottom and give her a bottle and burp her. I imagined that being a mother had to be the most wonderful experience in all the world. Daddy and Audrey, on the other hand, kept their distance. I'm thinking Audrey was that way because first, she didn't approve of the birth, and second, because she was just plain contrary.

4

My, oh, my, but Shirley was such a special child. Always smiling, good-natured, and as pretty as the day is long, she could charm the horns right off a billy goat. Her smile was pure sunshine and she quickly became the light of our lives. As an infant, she seldom cried and, if she did, you could bet your bottom dollar something was really wrong. Her diaper needed changing, her bottle was empty, or a pin was sticking her. By the time she was walking, she was into anything and everything. She wanted to help Mama cook, she wanted me to draw pictures for her, she wanted Betty Jean to play patty-cake and sing with her; there was no end to her interests. When she was two, Mama bought a coloring book filled with pictures of jungle animals, lions, tigers, giraffes, elephants, and such. The moment she got the coloring book, rather than coloring in the pictures, she started drawing the animals. I was amazed at how good she was. By the time she was three, we could see how smart she was. When she heard a children's song like

The Angel Years

"Twinkle, Twinkle Little Star" or "Itsy Bitsy Spider," she knew all the words upon hearing the song a single time.

I will always remember the day Mama sat down with Shirley at age four to teach her to read. By then, Shirley could already say her ABCs forwards and backwards. She had been reading and writing simple words and sentences for almost a year and sometimes she would ask me how to spell certain words or explain what that meant. So when Mama sat down with her that Sunday afternoon and opened a book of nursery rhymes, I was not surprised at what happened.

"Now we're going to start reading right here," Mama said, pointing to the opening lines in the book as Shirley sat in her lap.

Mama, trying to prime the pump, started to read.

"Now Old King Cole was a merry old soul…"

Then Shirley started to read.

"Now Old King Cole was a merry old soul and a merry old soul was he, he called for his pipe and he called for his bowl, and he called for his fiddlers three."

Not a single stumble or hesitation.

Then she continued.

"Every fiddler he had a fiddle, and a very fine fiddle had he; Oh there's none so rare, as can compare, with King Cole and his fiddlers three."

She stopped.

"Do you want me to read some more, Mama?" she asked, a look of pure innocence on her face.

Mama turned from the book and looked up at me. First, there was a look of bewilderment, then suddenly, she burst out laughing.

"My! My!" Mama said. "Now aren't you something?"

***

And Mama was right. Shirley knew things that kids her age were not supposed to know. For her fifth Christmas, Mama bought a toy tea set of white plastic cups, saucers, and sugar bowls, and Shirley loved to play hostess for me, Betty Jean, and Mama as guests. One by one, she would go around the table and pour water into our cups as we politely waited. Then she would go around the table asking if we wanted one lump of sugar or two. Once everyone's cup was prepared, she would seat herself.

"Now we will have our tea," she would say.

If anyone failed to bring their cup to their mouth without a "free pinkie," Shirley was quick to correct them. Once, when Mama didn't toe the line, Shirley instructed her: "Mama, please show a free pinkie."

Suddenly, Mama began giggling with delight at the ridiculousness of a five-year-old telling her how to drink tea. Moments later, Mama was quiet again and took another sip of tea, this time with a waving pinkie.

"Much better," Shirley said.

Where this child learned these things, none of us

The Angel Years

ever knew. We didn't have television and she wasn't old enough to read books about such things. I'll tell you, Shirley was something else.

***

As a small child, one of Shirley's favorite pastimes was playing with Truman. We had a family dog, a beagle with short legs, floppy ears, and sad eyes named Truman. Daddy named the dog Truman because he was born on the same day Truman officially beat Dewey in the 1948 presidential election. On the day of the election, several newspapers incorrectly announced Dewey had won, but, after all of the votes were counted, Truman was named the official winner. It was on that day that an old mongrel dog Mama had been feeding had three little pups in a hayrack at the barn. Once Daddy saw the puppies, he decided to keep the strongest and healthiest for a family dog and gave the others away. The one he kept he named Truman.

For hours on end, Shirley would play fetch in the front yard with Truman. She would laugh out loud as she watched him race across the yard to retrieve the stick she had thrown, then return it to her. In the summertime, when we went swimming in the river, Shirley would throw an old yellow rubber ball into the water, then watch delightedly as Truman swam into the river, took the ball in his mouth, and returned it to her. She loved Truman.

John Isaac Jones

***

Then there was the day Daddy tried to teach Shirley, at age five, to shuck corn. Every night, after Daddy came in from the fields, he would unharness the mules and bring them into the barn. He would put them in their stalls and feed each of them two forkfuls of hay and six ears of corn. On that particular day, Audrey and I were milking the cows in an adjacent stall while Shirley sat on the extra milking stool watching us.

After Daddy put up the mules, he stopped in front of the stall where we were milking.

"Audrey," he said. "Will you shuck the corn and feed the mules after the milking?"

"Why do I have to do it?" Audrey said. "When is Shirley going to learn to help around here?"

Daddy looked at Shirley.

"That's a good idea."

"Come on!" Daddy said, motioning for Shirley to follow him. "It's time you learned to shuck corn."

Shirley got up from the milking stool and followed Daddy to the corncrib at the end of the barn hallway. At the crib, Daddy opened the door and took out several ears of corn. Meanwhile, Mama was in the backyard hanging out clothes and was within earshot.

"Watch me!" Daddy said.

Shirley watched as Daddy took an ear of corn, expertly pulled back the husk, then broke off the stem

The Angel Years

and threw it into a waiting bucket.

"Now you do it," he said, handing an ear to Shirley.

Before taking it, she looked at it curiously, then back at Daddy. Finally, she took the ear of corn. Then, as she pulled back the husk, she saw a black wiggle worm and immediately threw the ear of corn on the ground in fright.

"It's a bug!" Shirley said. "I'm afraid of bugs."

Daddy picked up the ear of corn.

"It's just a wiggle worm," Daddy said, picking up the ear of corn. "He's not going to hurt you."

Daddy brushed away the black worm, then finished pulling back the husk.

"Now," he said, handing the ear of corn back to Shirley, "break off the stem!"

"No!" Shirley said. "I don't want to. I'm afraid."

"Now you listen to me, young lady," Daddy said. "It's time you learned to help around here. Finish shucking this!"

"No!" Shirley said, pulling her hands to her chest. "I don't want to! I'm afraid!"

For a moment, Daddy peered angrily at her. Then, suddenly, he grabbed her arm, pulled her to him, and started spanking her. Right away, Shirley started bawling.

That very moment, Mama, who was still hanging out clothes, heard Shirley wailing. She came running.

"Shirley!! Shirley!!" she called as she ran toward the barn.

Once she was in the barn hallway, she saw Daddy in front of the corn crib spanking Shirley.

"Stop!! Stop!!" Mama shouted.

She rushed forward and grabbed Daddy's spanking hand.

Daddy, still holding Shirley's arm, turned to her.

"This child is going to have to learn to work."

"No!" Mama said, still holding Daddy's hand. "Turn her loose."

When Daddy didn't immediately release Shirley's arm, Mama pulled Shirley's arm out of Daddy's grasp. Shirley, still wailing at the top of her lungs, rushed into Mama's arms.

"Baby, are you okay?" Mama said, holding her close and stroking her back. "Hush up now. Mama's here. Everything is going to be okay."

Shirley stopped crying.

Daddy peered helplessly at Mama.

"Look at you! All you're doing is raising a spoiled brat. She can learn to work like the rest of us."

"Not this one. This one is different." Mama glared angrily at him. "Don't you ever touch this baby again!"

"You just going to let her sit on her butt and look pretty all her life?"

"God has sent us a very special child," Mama said. "This child is going to be somebody in this family one of these days. I aim to keep her that way."

Daddy didn't reply. Quiet settled upon the barn again.

The Angel Years

"She's the little princess," Audrey said. "She thinks she's better than the rest of us…"

"You hush up too!!" Mama said.

Then, with Shirley clinging to her neck, Mama headed to the house.

***

Betty Jean was the first daughter to leave home. I always knew it was coming; I just didn't know when. In late May of 1959, she graduated Hawkins Valley High and got a job as a clerk at Brannon's Hardware over at the Crossroads. It was there she met Clyde Brannon, the younger brother of the owner, who was a mechanic in Tifton. He owned a motorcycle shop and, from the very first time I saw them together, I knew they were two of a kind.

I was sitting in the front porch swing one Saturday morning when I heard a motorcycle come roaring down the driveway toward our house. As it pulled up in the yard, I could see Clyde behind the handlebars, and Betty Jean, a package in her hand, perched comfortably behind him.

"Hi, Clyde," I said as he shut down the engine.

I knew Clyde. He had been in my history class in high school. He was decked out in black leather and heavy boots with silver buckles.

"Cornelia Johnson!" he said. "How you doing?"

"I'm doing fine, Clyde. How 'bout you?"

"Fine. Just dropping off your sister."

Betty Jean got off the motorcycle and turned to Clyde.

"I'll call you tomorrow."

We watched as Clyde fired up the motorcycle again and roared off down the driveway to the main highway.

"What you got in that package?"

"Come on!" Betty Jean said. "And I'll show you."

Moments later, we were in our room and Betty Jean started opening the package. Once open, she didn't reveal the contents immediately.

"Are you ready for this?"

"I'm ready."

Then she pulled a black leather jacket with an eagle on the back out of the package. She proudly held it up for me to see.

"Someday I'm going to wear this in public," she said. "I'm going to show the world who I am. The time is not right yet, but it will be."

Then she refolded the jacket and replaced it in the box.

"I'm going to hide this at the bottom of the closet. You won't say anything to Mama, will you?"

"No!"

"Thanks, Cornelia!" she said, hugging me. "I can always count on you."

***

The Angel Years

I knew Mama and Daddy, once they learned about it, would never approve of the path Betty Jean was on, but I also knew that, for Betty Jean, there was no turning back. Clyde was making a motorcycle girl out of her. One night, a few months later, she came to the family table with a small tattoo of a broken red heart on her arm.

Once everybody was seated and Mama said the blessing, Audrey wasted no time causing trouble.

"Daddy, look at the trash that Betty Jean has got on her arm."

Daddy leaned over and squinted through his glasses to see Betty Jean's arm.

"What you doing putting something like that on your arm? Ain't you got no sense?"

Even Mama took Daddy's side on this one.

"The good Lord gave us skin to cover and nourish our body. Not to be used to draw pictures."

"Oh, Mama!" Betty Jean said. "It's no big deal."

"You get that off your arm," Daddy said.

"I can't get it off," Betty Jean said. "It will be there for the rest of my life."

"You heard what I said," Daddy replied. "Get that trash off your arm or don't come back to this table."

Daddy peered angrily at her.

Instantly, Betty Jean got up from the table.

"Come back here!!" Daddy said.

As if she hadn't heard, Betty Jean left the house, slamming the door behind her. She disappeared for almost a month. Then one Saturday morning, she and Clyde roared into the front yard again. Daddy and Audrey were in town and me and Mama were sitting on the front porch peeling apples. Shirley was inside the house asleep.

"I've come to say good-bye, Mama," Betty Jean said. "Me and Clyde are leaving Hawkins Valley."

"Where you going?"

"Everywhere," she said. "I've come to get my things."

"Well, go on in there and get them. Your daddy's not here, so you'll be fine."

Moments later, Betty Jean and I were in our room.

"You leaving for good?"

She nodded as she started throwing clothes and personal items into a suitcase. Once the suitcase was filled, she pulled out the black leather jacket she had hidden in the closet two months earlier. Quickly, she put on the jacket then turned to look at herself in the mirror.

"I told you this day would come."

I nodded.

"I guess this is goodbye," she said. "Not sure if I'll ever see you again. Take care!"

"Will you write?"

"Maybe."

Then she hugged me and, suitcase in hand, headed for the door.

"Good luck," I said. "I love you."

"I love you too."

The Angel Years

Outside again, Betty Jean went straight to Mama.

"I'm sorry, Mama. I have to do what makes me happy."

"I understand. I hope you know what you're doing. Good luck! I love you!!"

"I love you too, Mama."

Then, decked out in her black jacket and holding the suitcase, she mounted the motorcycle. The engine roared to life and, in a cloud of dust, it sped off down the driveway.

Tears welled in Mama's eyes as she watched the motorcycle disappear into the distance.

"I always knew she was wild as a jack rabbit," Mama said to no one in particular, "but I didn't know what to do about it."

It was the last time we would ever see Betty Jean.

5

In the springtime, Shirley liked to go with me and Mama and Audrey and Truman to the river bottoms to pick blackberries. At the bend in the river, there was a big stand of wild blackberries that stretched for thirty, maybe forty yards along the river's edge and, by late April, the thorny bushes would be sagging with oodles and oodles of ripe, juicy fruit. When we went picking blackberries, we would get up early and trudge the half mile across the pasture to the river bottoms. Then Mama, Audrey, and I would get down on our knees, negotiate the stickers, and easily pick two or three gallons of fresh berries in a couple hours. Shirley complained that the thorns hurt her fingers, so Mama always gave her the easiest task, holding the bucket while we picked.

One day in the spring of 1959, some six months before Shirley started school, we were just finishing up our blackberry picking, when Mama said we had to stop because a big rain was coming. In the east, the sky was

The Angel Years

dark with heavy thunderclouds.

"Come on!" Mama said. "We better run for the house. If we don't, we're going to get soaking wet."

Mama grabbed one bucketful of blackberries and I grabbed the other and we started running. By the time we reached the house, rain was coming down in buckets. When I mounted the front porch steps, I saw Daddy had already come in and was sitting in the porch swing. Moments later, the entire family was sitting on the front porch, quietly watching the rain come down in buckets. From time to time, bright flashes of lightning streaked across the sky and huge claps of thunder rattled the tin roof above our heads.

"Have you ever noticed that you always hear thunder, then see the lightning," Audrey said. "The thunder causes the lightning."

"No," Shirley said. "It's just the opposite. When lightning shoots through the air, it warms up the air around it and causes it to explode. Thunder is what you hear as the air around the lightning explodes. Lightning comes first."

Everybody was quiet.

"The electrostatic particles collide together to create the sound of thunder," Shirley continued. "The thunder we hear is the collision of those electrostatic particles."

Everybody in the family looked from one to the other.

"What kind of particles?" Daddy said.

"Electrostatic particles," Shirley said. "Tiny little

new particles of energy that have electronic charges."

"Oh Lord, Honey," Mama said. "I don't know what you talking about."

Finally, Daddy looked over at Shirley.

"Where did you learn that?"

"I don't know," Shirley said. "I just know it."

"I been telling y'all this child is special," Mama said.

For a long moment, everyone was quiet again.

"The little princess thinks she knows everything," Audrey said. "If you got any questions, just ask her."

Suddenly, Audrey stood up, glared at Shirley, then went into the house, slamming the screen door behind her.

"Mama," Shirley said. "Can I have some more ice cream and peach cobbler?"

"Yeah, but you need to get those wet clothes off first."

Mama stood up and took the two buckets of blackberries in hand. Then, with her head, she motioned for me to open the screen door.

"You're spoiling that child rotten," Daddy said as I held the door.

Mama peered at him.

"I told you! This is my child and I'm going to raise her the way I want to."

Then she turned to Shirley.

"Come on, baby, let's go inside."

The Angel Years
***

As Shirley got older, she wouldn't do farm work, but she liked to tag along with me and Mama while we were doing ours. Lots of times, she would go with us to the barn to milk the cows. While we were milking, she liked to play on the old tire swing at the end of the "cow lane." Years before, Daddy had built an old tire swing under an oak tree at the end of what we called the cow lane. The cow lane was a fenced stretch of about 50 yards from the barn to the main pasture and the cows had to pass down this narrow passageway to come to the barn.

Late one afternoon, when Shirley was seven, me and Mama were milking the cows and Shirley was swinging when she suddenly started screaming at the top of her lungs.

"Mama! Mama!"

I jumped up from my milking and peered down the cow lane. I could see Shirley, frightened out of her wits, tearing down the lane.

When she saw me, she rushed into my arms.

"Shirley! What's wrong?"

"A ghost jumped out at me!"

"A ghost?" Mama said. "What ghost?"

"Look!" Shirley said, pointing into the darkness. "It's still chasing me!! Look!"

Moments later, I saw a white, human-looking form coming down the lane toward us. Once it drew closer, I could see it was Audrey. She had an old sheet wrapped around her head and body and was laughing her head off.

"What you doing scaring this baby like that?" Mama said.

Audrey threw the sheet over her head and rushed at Shirley again.

"Boo!! I'm a ghost! Boo!! Boo!"

"No! No!" Shirley said, clinging tighter. "Tell her to go away."

I shoved Audrey away.

"Now you leave her alone," Mama said. "And I mean now!!!"

Audrey removed the sheet from her head.

"Oh, Mama, I was just having some fun," Audrey said. "The little princess is scared of her own shadow."

***

In September of 1960, when Mama took Shirley to be registered for school, the health department nurse said she had to see a birth certificate before she could give her the vaccinations. Mama explained that Shirley was adopted and presented the falsified birth certificate she had received with the falsified adoption papers. The nurse took down all of the information, then handed it back to Mama without question.

Once Shirley started the first grade, she was just as special to the teachers as she was to us. In the second grade, she got a "Best Reader" commendation from her

The Angel Years

teacher and a certificate for having grades of 100 on all of her spelling tests. She was the most popular member of her class, and her fellow students voted her president of the second grade. When the school sponsored a finger-painting contest, Shirley's entry of a setting sun was the winner in the grammar school division. This meant Shirley, as a second grader, had won out over lots of fifth and sixth graders.

***

When Mama took Shirley to school to begin the third grade, the principal called Mama into her office.

"This child's mind is far ahead of the other students in the third grade," she said. "I suggest she begin the fourth grade this year."

"I know how smart she is," Mama said, "but I want her to grow up around children her own age, so let's go ahead and put her in the third grade. It will be better in the long run…"

"As you wish," the principal replied.

***

On Sunday afternoons, Shirley liked to tag along with me when I went down to the catfish pond to paint birds. Most of the time, she seemed like a normal child, but other times, it was like she was from another world. On one particular Sunday in late September of 1962, I was putting the final touches on a blue jay when I saw her coming down the path to the pond. When she arrived, she walked right up to my painting and studied it for a several moments without saying a word.

"There is such a glory and beauty in nature," she said finally. "Everything in the world works so perfectly with everything else. Photosynthesis and plant life. The cycle of rain. The rhythm of the tides. The movement of the planets around the sun. How could anyone say there is no God?"

I stopped painting and peered at her.

"Where did you ever hear a word like that?"

"Like what?"

"Like photosynthesis."

"I just know it…"

I returned to my painting and didn't pursue the subject further.

Shirley took a seat on the quilt at my feet and gazed quietly across the pond for several minutes.

"I can understand why you love painting nature so much," she said finally. "It's a celebration of nature's beauty. Once, when I was nineteen years old, I knew a woman who spent endless hours at the ocean painting shore birds. She could get all of these different shades of blue in her work."

"Shirley, you've never been nineteen years old."

"Yes I have."

"When?"

"Many years ago."

The Angel Years

"Honey, you're only eight years old now. How could you ever have been nineteen?"

She smiled.

"Someday I'll tell you."

We were quiet for a moment.

"Someday I'll be famous," she continued. "I'll have lots of money and I'll get awards and they will have parades in my honor."

I couldn't believe what she was saying.

"You seem so sure about it."

"Oh, it will happen."

"How do you know things like that?"

"I just know."

I tried to pursue the subject, but she refused to talk further of it.

***

One night in the fall of 1965, Shirley, at age 11, announced at the dinner table that her teacher told the class there was a woman over in Albany who taught singing and acting classes.

"Her name is Mrs. Benefield and she teaches the lessons every Saturday afternoon for three hours. I want you to start taking me over there for lessons."

"How much are the lessons?" Mama asked.

"Ten dollars."

"Ten dollars?" Daddy said. "We can't afford that."

"Did the teacher say the woman had experience as

an actress?" Mama asked.

"The teacher said Mrs. Benefield had been an actress and singer on Broadway for several years."

"We'll go over next Saturday and talk to her."

"Now, Ila, we can't be throwing away our money for acting lessons," Daddy said. "That money could be better put to work for other things."

"Like what?"

"I need barbed wire and fence posts for the lower pasture."

"I'll get the money for the lessons."

"How?"

"I'll figure out something."

Daddy shook his head helplessly.

"This child is going to drive us into the poorhouse."

Mama turned to Shirley.

"Don't worry," she said. "On Saturday, we're going over to Albany and talk to this woman."

***

So Shirley started her acting and singing lessons. Every Saturday afternoon, Mama would take her over to Albany to meet with Mrs. Benefield. Once the lessons started, Shirley had me and Mama acting out scenes from famous plays. In particular, I remember Mama, with a wig on her head, trying to play the role of Wendy in *Peter Pan* while Shirley pranced around as Peter. When Daddy came in and saw us, he burst out laughing.

The Angel Years

"Y'all have gone plumb crazy."

Audrey, as usual, not only wanted no part of it, but mocked Shirley every chance she got. When Shirley would show up at the dinner table each night, Audrey would get in her licks.

"Oh, look who's here!" Audrey would say. "The famous movie star has arrived to show us how wonderful she is. Let's all applaud her royal highness!"

"Now you leave Shirley alone," Mama said. "All this has got nothing to do with you."

For two years, Mama took Shirley over to Albany every Saturday morning for her acting and singing lessons with Mrs. Benefield. At night, while Mama and Daddy were in the living room listening to the radio, we would hear Shirley in her room singing "Goodnight Ladies," "Old Black Joe," or "Alexander's Ragtime Band." Night after night, her singing would drone on and on. After a while, the other members of the family knew the words to "Goodnight Ladies" as well as Shirley. I even found myself singing it during idle moments. On Saturday nights, when Daddy tried to listen to the news and the Grand Ole Opry on the radio, he would turn up the volume to drown out Shirley's singing.

***

One afternoon in the late summer of 1966, Shirley said something in idle conversation I would always remember. By late August of that year, the purple hull peas were hanging in thick bunches on the vines and were ripe for picking. During these times, me, Mama, Audrey, and Shirley would get up early in the morning and, together with Truman, go to the fields, and pick peas until about midday. Once we had several bushel baskets filled, we would lug them back home, sit on the back porch, and shell peas for the rest of the day. Me, Mama and Audrey would sit in a circle around the unshelled peas, take handfuls into our laps to shell, then, once they were shelled, throw the husks into a separate empty basket. When you shell purple hull peas, you get a dark purplish stain on the palm of your hand that lasts for several days. After Shirley told Mama that she didn't want to get the purple stain on her hands, Mama gave her the job of emptying the basket of husks once it had been filled. Now, shelling peas is a really boring task and, to pass the time, Mama always like to reminisce about her younger years.

"When I was a young girl growing up in Tifton," Mama said, "I had my dreams. I wanted to be a public speaker and have people come and listen to me talk. I wanted people to know me and know who I was. Not all over the world, but I did want people in Hawkins Valley to know me and to know my name."

She stopped, took another handful of peas into her lap, then began shelling again.

"Then, when I met your daddy," she continued, "everything changed. We got married, set up a home,

The Angel Years

and then you kids started coming. My dream ended when I married your daddy. Marriage really changes your life."

We were quiet for several minutes.

"Audrey," I said. "Think you'll ever get married?"

She didn't answer at first.

"You know the old saying," she said finally. "Boys don't make passes at girls who wear glasses."

"That's not true," Mama said. "Women that wear glasses get married all the time."

"No," Audrey said. "I won't get married until I have my eye operation and don't have to wear glasses."

"Someday you'll get your eye operation," I said.

"Where is the money going to come from?" Audrey replied.

"I'll get the money," Shirley said. "Someday I'll give you the money to get your operation."

Audrey laughed out loud.

"Ha-ha!" she said. "The little princess is going to give me the money for my eye operation? That'll be the day."

We were quiet again.

Audrey, her lap full of unshelled peas, turned to me.

"What about you? When are you going to get married? You're 27 and still single."

"I don't know. The right man just hasn't come along."

"Why didn't you like Nathan McCartney?" Audrey said. "You went out with him several times."

"Nathan? Oh, I could never marry a mechanic. I want to marry a man with some education. Some refinement."

"Wendell Campbell was sweet on you in high school," Audrey continued. "He's a teacher at the college over in Tifton now. He would have been a good catch."

I didn't answer at first.

"I don't think I would make a good wife," I said finally. "I just don't think I could take a man bossing me around all the time. I don't think there's a man alive I could love more than my paintings."

A long silence as we shelled peas.

"Has it got anything to do with Lawrence Calloway?" Mama asked.

"Who is Lawrence Calloway," Shirley asked.

"Cornelia fell in love with Lawrence Calloway during high school," Mama said. "they dated for almost two years and planned to be married then, when he went off to college…"

"Mama!" I said suddenly. "Do we have to talk about this?"

"Shirley needs to know about Lawrence…." Mama said.

"I don't want to talk about it" I said.

Audrey, of course, had to get in her two cents worth.

"Cornelia and Lawrence fell in love in high school, then when he went up to north Georgia to go to college, he met somebody else and left Cornelia holding the bag."

"You've got a big mouth!" I said.

"Maybe so, but the truth is the truth and it should be told."

We were quiet again.

The bushel basket that held the pea husks was full now and Shirley picked it up, emptied the husks into a nearby trash bin, and replaced it for us to use again.

"You'll be married someday, Cornelia," Shirley said as she replaced the now empty bushel basket in its original position. "And you'll have to learn to cook Italian food. Especially ravioli."

All of us stopped shelling peas, startled at Shirley's comment.

Audrey burst out laughing.

"The little princess has lost her marbles."

She turned to me.

"Hey, Sister Cornelia, didn't you know you got to learn to cook Italian food? Don't you think it's time you learned to cook ravioli?"

Once Audrey's mocking laughter ended, I turned to Shirley.

"Ravioli? You mean those little squares of pasta with meat inside?"

"That's right."

"Now why in the world would I ever want to learn to cook ravioli?"

"It will happen."

I laughed at the thought.

"Shirley, I love you, but sometimes you just don't make any sense," I said.

"You'll see."

***

That night, as I lay awake in bed, my mind wandered back to that conversation. The real reason I wasn't married was because I was afraid of love. My experience with Lawrence had left too many scars on my heart and I wasn't sure if I wanted to ever go through it again. Yes, I wanted to be married and have children someday, but, after what happened between me and Lawrence, my heart always raised warning flags every time the opportunity for love approached. It needed lots of healing after Lawrence. As I drifted off to sleep that night, I laughed out loud at Shirley's comment about me learning to cook ravioli.

***

Somehow, way down deep, I had always suspected that Shirley was sent to us from another world, but my suspicions were not confirmed until the winter of 1966 when Truman, the family dog, took sick. One night, at the dinner table, Daddy announced that he had taken Truman to the veterinarian.

"You paid good money to a veterinarian to look at that old dog?"

The Angel Years

"Not exactly," Daddy said. "He did the examination for free. He owed me some money for some field work I did for him last spring."

"What did he say about Truman?" Mama asked.

"He's got a cancer in his stomach and he's not going to live more than a few days."

"Oh, no!" Shirley, who was twelve, replied. "We can't let Truman die."

"There's nothing we can do," Daddy said. "He's eighteen years old. That's a good long life for a dog."

"No!" Shirley said. "I want to see him. I want to make him healthy."

"You can't make him healthy. The vet said he would be dead in three days."

"Where is he?"

"He's in the barn."

Instantly, Shirley pushed her chair back from the table.

"Finish your meal first," Mama said.

"No. I want to see Truman. Now!"

She turned to me.

"Cornelia, will you go to the barn with me?"

"Sure."

So we took a flashlight and started out the back door to the barn.

Truman was lying on an old blanket that had been thrown across a pile of hay. Food was in his bowl, but had not been touched. When he saw us, he was too weak to raise his head, so he just looked up at us with those sad, weary eyes.

"Poor Truman," Shirley said as she bent down to examine him. "He's sick. Very sick, but I'm going to make him well."

"What are you going to do?"

"You must never reveal what I'm about to do. Promise?"

"Promise."

Shirley stood in front of the dog and held both hands over her head with index fingers fully extended. Then she brought her hands down together in a sudden thrusting motion. As her hands swept downward, bolts of fiery light emanated from her fingertips and, instantly, Truman's entire body was enveloped by a luminous white light as if a giant electrical charge was being passed through it. For several seconds, the dog's body trembled in this state of electrified illumination, then Shirley threw her hands up again and the glowing aura disappeared.

For a moment, the dog looked around as if he was confused or in a daze. Then he stood up, went to the bowl, and started eating. We watched as he finished the food in his bowl.

"Come on," Shirley said. "Let's go to the house."

Instantly, the dog, frisky as ever, fell in lockstep behind us and followed us to the house.

"Truman is just fine!" Shirley announced when we walked back inside where the family was still eating.

Daddy gazed at her in disbelief.

The Angel Years

"Fine? Where is he now?"

"He's on the back porch."

Daddy's face turned into a scowl, then unable contain himself, he got up from the table and went to the back porch. When he opened the back door, Truman ran to him and began rubbing his body against his leg to be petted.

Daddy shook his head in disbelief.

"What is God's name did you do to that dog? I've never in my life seen anything like that. I thought he was a goner. I guess miracles just happen sometimes."

6

In the fall of 1967, at age 13, Shirley entered the seventh grade at Hawkins Valley High. During the second week, fellow students voted her president of the class. At the dinner table that night, she told Mama she wanted to start wearing store-bought dresses to school.

"Why do you need store-bought dresses?"

"I can't be class president in a flour sack dress, Mama. It just doesn't look right."

"Let me see what I can do," Mama said.

"Ila, we can't afford it."

"I don't care," Mama said. "This child is going to get what she needs to make it in this world."

"Where are you going to get the money?"

"I don't know."

***

Two days later, on a Saturday morning, me and Mama went into Albany to the pawn shop. Mama had a

The Angel Years

brooch with a red ruby inside that her mother had given her when she died. Mother asked the man to give her one hundred dollars for the brooch, but he wouldn't go higher than seventy-five dollars. Finally, Mama took it. Then we went to Holcomb's Clothing Store and Mama spent forty-eight dollars for five new dresses and two pairs of new shoes for Shirley.

That night, while Shirley was trying on the new dresses in her bedroom, Audrey came in and had a raving fit.

"It's not fair!" she shouted. "Me and Cornelia had to wear flour sack dresses all the way through high school. Now the little princess gets store-bought dresses and shoes in junior high."

Mama didn't say a word. She turned, went to Audrey, put her in a headlock, and started leading her out of the bedroom.

"Mama!" Audrey screamed. "You're hurting my neck."

"I'm going to hurt something else if you don't get out of here."

At the bedroom door, Mama released her, then shoved her through the open doorway. Defiantly, Audrey stood in the doorway, glaring at Mama.

"Now don't you come back until I'm finished."

Then she slammed the door in Audrey's face.

Throughout the rest of her junior and senior high school days at Hawkins Valley High, Shirley wore store-bought dresses.

***

That same year, Shirley wrote a little play titled *The Gallant Knight* about a handsome prince who won the hand of the beautiful princess after slaying the mighty dragon. When she showed it to Miss Elizabeth Poe, her seventh-grade teacher, the teacher was very impressed and decided to have the class perform it. After the class acted out the play, with Shirley in the role of the princess, Miss Poe sent a note home to Mama that read "Shirley is a truly gifted child."

In the fall of 1969, Shirley turned fifteen and started high school. By then, Miss Poe, the seventh-grade teacher who had staged her play two years earlier, was the drama coach at Hawkins Valley High. Every year, the school put on a production and, that year, they were staging *Joan of Arc*, the story of the teenage girl who led French Troops against the English at the Battle of Orleans. Despite numerous try-outs, Miss Poe was unable to find a suitable actress for the lead. Then remembering Shirley's play, she asked her former student to try out. The very instant she saw Shirley outfitted and reciting lines, she was sold, and Shirley was cast in the lead.

***

The dress rehearsal for the Hawkins Valley High

The Angel Years

production of *Joan of Arc* was held on the night on March 22, 1970 in the high school auditorium. Mama and I accompanied Shirley to the event. After it was finished, me, Mama, and Shirley were leaving, when Miss Poe pulled Shirley aside.

"I wanted to tell you that my brother Thomas, a theatrical producer in Atlanta, will be in the audience tomorrow night to see your performance. I've been telling him about your many talents and I wanted him to see you on stage with his own eyes. He is just one more reason you should give tomorrow night's performance your very best effort."

"Oh, I will," Shirley said. "I'll give it my best."

***

When *Joan of Arc* was staged the following night, it was a big hit. Mother and I attended and, as they say, Shirley "brought down the house." She got three curtain calls and, afterward, a huge mob of students rushed backstage to congratulate her. Finally, once the celebrations were finished, we started to leave. Outside, in front of the school, we saw Miss Poe.

"Was your brother here?" Shirley asked.

"Oh yes. He was here, but I didn't get a chance to talk to him after the performance. I'll talk to him next week."

***

During school the following week, Miss Poe called Shirley out of class to come to her office. She said she had finally had a chance to talk to her brother and he had greatly admired her performance. After explaining that her brother and another producer were planning to bring *Joan of Arc* to the big screen, Miss Poe said he had asked her to have Mama give him a call. He wanted to talk to her about Shirley coming to Atlanta for some screen tests.

The following morning, Mama called Mr. Thomas Poe and they made arrangements for Shirley to go to Atlanta. That night at the dinner table, Mama relayed the details of the call.

"Horace, do you want to go to Atlanta with me and Shirley for her movie tests?"

"Ila, you know I don't know nothing about all that. All this acting and singing business has been you and Shirley's doings from the first."

Mama looked at Audrey.

"I'm not interested," Audrey said. "Why would I want to go watch the little princess preen herself like a peacock?"

Mama turned to me.

"Cornpone?"

"I'd love to go."

***

The Angel Years

Me, Mama, and Shirley were in Atlanta for four days. The movie company put us up in a fancy hotel with king-size beds and chandeliers in the lobby. We ate food I'd never heard of. Potatoes au gratin, beef Stroganoff, filet mignon, and some other dishes I couldn't pronounce their names. That night, from the hotel window, I could see all the bright lights and tall buildings in Atlanta.

The next morning, we went to Shamrock Productions, a movie studio in downtown Atlanta where they were going to do the screen tests. During the tests, Shirley would spend hours getting her face and hair done, then they would dress her up in different costumes and she would sit in front of the camera for hours while the director tried this or that shot or some new angle. It was all very interesting. At night, Mama would go through the script with Shirley, practicing and memorizing her lines.

Finally, at the end of the third day, Mr. Poe, a tall, unsmiling man with dark hair, sad eyes, and a mustache, told Mama he wanted to sign Shirley up to play the lead in the movie version of *Joan of Arc*.

"I want to start shooting in Northern California in two weeks," he said. "Who is her agent?"

Mama stopped at the word.

"Agent? She doesn't have an agent."

"She's got to have an agent to draw up and oversee her contract," he said. "And probably a chaperone. You realize that, as a professional actress, she will be constantly traveling and will need personal and professional supervision."

"Supervision?"

"Yes, she's not of age," he said. "She'll need someone to care for her personal needs and schooling while she is travelling."

"Lordy mercy, I don't know nothing about movie contracts. I'll going to call my cousin Troy and get some advice."

Mama had a first cousin named Troy Franklin she had grown up with in Tifton. The oldest son of her sister Marjorie, Troy was in his late fifties, was a graduate of the University of Georgia law school, and had a successful practice in Atlanta. That afternoon, Mama gave him a call.

***

When we went into Troy's office that afternoon, he looked a little pudgier and a little grayer than I remembered him at Grandma's funeral seventeen years earlier. At age 58, he had a round face and a quick smile. Every time I saw him, he reminded me of a used car salesman. He liked to shake hands, had a toothy smile, and loved to slap people on the back.

"My! My! Cornelia!" he said when he saw me. "You're all grown up now. And you're so pretty."

Then Mama introduced Shirley.

"And this is my pride and joy. She's the reason

The Angel Years

we're here for this meeting."

Over the next few minutes, Mama explained that Shirley had an offer to star in a film production of *Joan of Arc*. She relayed all of the details of what Mr. Poe had said and finished by saying the production was due to start shooting in northern California in two weeks.

"I can be her agent," Troy said, "but we're going to have to work fast. How old is Shirley?"

"She'll be sixteen in September."

"Are you going to travel with her and be a stage mother?"

"Me? Travel with her?"

"She's not of age. She's going to have to have an adult to attend to her personal needs, take care of her appointments, schedule her school sessions, and serve as her publicist. Are you going to do all that?"

"Heavens no! I couldn't leave the farm."

"What about Cornelia?"

"Oh, she couldn't leave the farm either."

"Then you're going to need a child entertainer coordinator."

Mama peered at him for a moment, not knowing what to say next.

"Where could I find someone like that?"

"I think I know just the person," Troy said. "I'm going to give her a call and we'll have dinner with her tonight."

"What's her name?"

"Sophia. Sophia LaFollette. She's French-

Canadian."

***

Sophia LaFollette was a small, boyish-looking woman in her early thirties with hay-colored hair and alert blues eyes. She was wearing one of those little round beret hats that you see French painters in magazines wearing when standing in front of an easel. Immediately, I could sense the worldliness, the city manners, and the quiet confidence in her bearing. Even before she started speaking with a slight French accent, I could see she would be perfect for Shirley.

Over dinner, Shirley asked her questions. Sophia said, in her last job, she had been the personal assistant to Clarice Sinclair, the famous Canadian opera singer, for three years. Together, they had travelled across Canada several times with an opera company.

"What did you do before that?" Shirley said.

"I was personal assistant to Baby Jane Campbell, the child actress who starred in *Salad Days* and *One More Take*."

"Oh, yes," Shirley said. "I've heard of her. She's in Europe now on the London stage. How old is she now?"

"She's thirteen now. I was her personal assistant for five years."

"From ages eight to thirteen?"

"That's correct."

From that point on, I could see the deal was done.

The Angel Years

Over the next hour, Shirley and Sophia were chatting, laughing, and sharing life experiences as if they had been life-long friends. When we parted that night, each of us hugged Sophia and Troy said he would call her the following morning with Shirley's decision.

"So what do you think?" Troy asked Shirley as we rode in the taxi back to the hotel.

"She will be perfect," Shirley said. "I couldn't be happier."

Mama turned to her.

"Remember, you're going to be with her all the time now. It won't be me and Cornpone with you every day. All you'll have is this little French woman."

"She'll be fine, Mama."

We were quiet for a moment.

"Then I'm going to meet with Shamrock executives tomorrow," Troy said. "I'll draw up the contracts and Shirley and Sophia will leave for California in two weeks."

"Everything sure is moving fast," Mama said.

"That's the way these things are," Troy replied.

The following morning, we checked out of the hotel and said good-bye to Troy. Before we got into a taxi to go to the bus station, Troy had some parting words for Mama.

"Ila, you know this could be big. Really big!"

"I hope so."

7

So Shirley's movie career was on its way. Over the first year, while she was working on the *Joan of Arc* movie, I talked to her four, maybe five times. Mama talked to her every week or two, so, between us, we kept a close watch on Shirley's pursuit of Hollywood stardom. When Shirley called, Mama would hold the receiver between us so we could both listen and talk at the same time. We loved to hear her talk about making movies. It all sounded so glamourous and exciting. Also, early on, we learned to not talk about Shirley's career in front of Daddy or Audrey. Neither had an interest in her success. In fact, Audrey, if Mama and I started to discuss Shirley in her presence, would get up and leave.

In April, the first time I talked to her, she was in northern California shooting village scenes, which focused on Joan of Arc's childhood days in the French countryside.

The Angel Years

"Making movies is not everything it appears to the outside world," she said. "Some days I'll be in makeup for two or three hours to shoot a scene, which will only be a couple minutes of film."

"At least you're getting to see the world. Are you happy?"

"Oh yes, very happy. I'm doing what I love."

When the conversation ended, I told Mama we were going to have to start a scrapbook of Shirley's career. She agreed.

When we talked to her again the following September, she was in "the flatlands of Eastern Canada" shooting scenes that recreated the famous battle at Orleans, France, where Joan, at age 14, had led the French Army against the English.

"Three of the last four days I have spent on a horse. I don't like horses. They have an unpleasant smell and I'm afraid of them."

At Thanksgiving, she said they were filming the final scenes of the episode, where Joan is tried, convicted of heresy, and burned at the stake.

"Oh, how terrible," I said.

"It's a very sad ending. The director says we will be finished in the next two weeks and the studio wants to release it on Christmas Day. Once it goes into theaters, we'll see the reviews and box office returns. Then we'll know where my career is going."

"Have you been doing interviews with the Hollywood magazines?" I asked.

"Oh, yes. Loads and loads. Sophia and I did four just last week."

***

In early January of the new year, I couldn't wait to get to Snellgrove's to see what articles the movie magazines had about Shirley. I went through every page of all five magazines and I saw only one little story and a small photo of Shirley buried deep inside. The photo, which was taken from a battle scene in the movie, didn't even look like Shirley. Her hair was cut short like a boy's and, with all of the makeup around her eyes, she looked like everybody but my baby sister. In spite of the poor picture, the article praised her performance. I bought a copy and read it to Mama at the dinner table that night.

"Shirley Temple Johnson is the newest rising star on the Hollywood horizon," the article said. "Her performance as Joan of Arc in the new Christmas release is a jewel of a performance. She brings an energy and a passion to the role, which stands head and shoulders above Joan of Arcs of the past. An Oscar nomination could well be in store for this newcomer."

When I finished reading the article, Mama applauded. Daddy didn't blink an eyelash. He just kept eating his meat loaf and green beans. When I started

The Angel Years

reading, Audrey had gotten up and left the table without finishing her meal. There was no end to the jealousy in that girl.

In late February, me and Mama went to Valdosta to see the *Joan of Arc* movie. Mama had been saving her butter and egg money for a month so we could go. As I sat there chewing popcorn and watching the movie, I was so happy. I couldn't believe that was my baby sister Shirley up there on the big screen. It was like a dream come true. Mama cried like a little baby during the scene where Joan was burned at the stake.

It would be another two months before we talked to her again. One Sunday afternoon in late April, me and Mama were washing clothes when we heard the phone ring.

"Good news," Shirley began. "After the studio saw the *Joan of Arc* box office receipts for January, February, and March, Mr. Leonard Cohen, the president of Shamrock, called Troy. Tomorrow, we're going to his office to sign a contract for a four-picture deal."

"Four pictures?" I said. "That's great!"

"Looks like I'm on my way."

"I couldn't be happier for you," Mama replied. "Are you coming to visit?"

"No time for that. I'm going to Idaho next week to start filming a western movie."

"What's the title?" I asked

"*The Man from Cheyenne*. It's the story of a sheriff, who, after being accused of murder, goes on the run with a school teacher."

***

In late June of 1971, Shirley was in Montana finishing up *The Man From Cheyenne*.

"I had forgotten how much I hated horses," she began. "During one scene, the horse I was riding threw me and I sprained my ankle. Oh, it was so painful. Over the next two weeks, we had to shoot scenes where I was sitting down while my ankle healed. I'm fine now. I hate horses."

"How do you like making a western?"

"Too many guns and violence. Too much blood. This movie has four gunfight scenes. There's already enough killing and violence in this world. I'll be glad when it's over."

When *The Man From Cheyenne* was released the following November, I went through all of the December issues of the movie magazines at Snellgrove's. Not a single mention of my baby sister. When the movie came to Valdosta, Mama and I didn't go see it. We didn't have the money. What's more, neither one of us liked westerns.

***

The Angel Years

In the early spring of 1972, Shirley began work on the third movie. The title was *Executioner's Song*, a courtroom drama about a holdout on a jury that was considering the fate of a man who, from all the evidence, appeared to be guilty.

"I didn't like this film from the start," she said. "I let Troy talk me into it because he said the studio really wanted me in the role of the only female juror. Courtroom stories are so dry and have no heart-felt feelings. I have no interest in trials and lawyers and objections. Such things bore me to death."

She stopped.

"But there is one silver living."

"What's that?"

"I'm working with Rock Hamilton. He is playing one of the jurors."

"Rock Hamilton?" I screamed into the phone. "The most handsome man in all of Hollywood?"

"That's the one."

I could feel myself swoon.

"Oh, Shirley! I would just like to look into his eyes."

"One more thing."

"What's that?"

"We're dating."

That took the cake. My sister Shirley was not only a rising Hollywood star, but she was dating the most handsome actor in Hollywood. Talk about hitting the jackpot!

"Oh, Shirley," I said. "I'm so happy for you."

I was jumping with joy when I hung up the phone. I knew Shirley was having a romance with Rock Hamilton before the Hollywood magazines.

***

At Christmas of 1973, there was more news of Shirley and Rock.

"Oh, Cornelia," she began. "Now don't faint when I tell you this."

"I won't. What is it?"

"The next movie I'm making is a romantic comedy. I have the female lead and guess who is playing the male lead."

"Rock Hamilton!"

"You got it. We start shooting in two weeks in Los Angeles."

"You mean you'll get to kiss him?"

"I'm already kissing him for real. We're dating. Remember?"

"Oh yeah. I forgot."

"What's the name of the new movie?"

"*A Kiss in the Dark*. It's the story of a secretary in New York who falls in love with her boss, but they can't get married because her ex-husband won't give her a divorce. I read the script. It's going to be lots of fun. No guns. No killing. No horses. Only laughter and good clean fun."

The Angel Years

I had stars in my eyes when I hung up the phone. Here I was a grown woman, over thirty-four years old, acting like a teenager as I watched my baby sister's rise to Hollywood stardom.

***

When *Kiss in the Dark* was released in May, 1974, it was a huge hit. With the release, Shamrock announced that not only were the leads two of the brightest stars in Hollywood, but they had fallen in love during production of the movie. When I saw the story announcing the release, I wanted to write the editors and tell them they had it wrong. Shirley and Rock had fallen in love during the making of *Executioner's Song*, not *Kiss in the Dark*, but I didn't.

In October, when the Motion Picture Association announced that year's winners, Shirley won the award for best actress. This meant that the November issues of the movie magazines were going to have lots of stories about her.

***

On November 1, 1974, me and Mama went to Albany and straight to Snellgrove's. At the magazine section, I could see that the new issues were still bundled up and had not been placed on the rack. At the front of the store, I saw Mr. Snellgrove, a thin, middle-aged man with balding hair and glasses, making change at the cash register.

"Mr. Snellgrove," I said, "can you open the new movie magazines so me and Mama can see them?"

"Why are you in such a rush?"

"I want to read all about my baby sister."

"Who is your sister?"

"Shirley Temple Johnson."

He peered at me for a long moment.

"Why, I remember her," he said. "Didn't she used to come in here with you? As I recall, she was a little blonde girl, very pretty, always smiling and happy."

"That's Shirley. She won a big award for best actress."

"I'm going to have to talk to the mayor about this."

Then he returned to the task at hand.

"Come on. I'll open these bundles and put the copies in the rack."

Shirley was on the front cover of all five movie magazines. Mama bought three and I bought two. It was for our scrapbook.

Two months later, when *Kiss in the Dark* came to the theater in Valdosta, me and Mama pooled our money and went to see it. It was a comedy, but me and Mama were so proud to see Shirley on the big screen that we cried all the way through it. We were so happy.

***

The Angel Years

By the spring of 1975, Shirley was famous all over the world. On Saturdays, when me and Mama went to Albany, we couldn't wait to get to Snellgrove's. Some Saturdays, we would see ten to fifteen different photos and stories about her. She would be at a premiere, a charity event, signing autographs, posing for photos, or vacationing with Rock Hamilton in places like Monaco or Bermuda. One Saturday, I almost fell over when I saw a photo of myself in *Movie Day* magazine. It had a story about Shirley's childhood and there was an Easter photo that Mama had made of Shirley and me at church. Shirley, who was seven or eight, was all dressed up in her Easter outfit and sitting in my lap. As I stared at the photo, I was so proud. Now, because of Shirley, I was becoming a celebrity myself. On the street, people I didn't know would come up to me and say: "Aren't you Shirley Temple Johnson's sister?" When I answered, they would reply: "Oh, I just love her movies." Old high school friends would see me and ask, "When was the last time you saw Shirley?" or "I'll bet you're proud of your sister…" Oh yes, I was proud beyond words.

***

In May, there was a front-page picture of Shirley and a story in the *Albany Herald*. The headline read: 'Local girl makes good in Hollywood.' It talked all about Shirley's achievements, her childhood, and her days at Hawkins Valley High. In the article, Miss

Elizabeth Poe, who was still the drama teacher, went on and on about how she always knew Shirley was destined for great things. Mama cut the article out of the paper, placed it in a picture frame, and put it on the mantel over the fireplace in the living room.

***

One afternoon in late June, two weeks after the newspaper article appeared, a strange car pulled into our front yard. It was a big black sedan and a smallish man in his early fifties, clean-shaven and well-dressed with a noticeable paunch, got out and strode across the yard. He stopped at the bottom of the porch steps when he saw Mama standing in the doorway.

"Mrs. Horace Johnson?"

"Yes, sir! That's me."

"I'm Thomas Booker, the Mayor of Albany. Can I speak with you?"

"Sure. Come on up and have a seat on the porch. I'll fix you a glass of iced tea."

Once he was comfortably situated on the porch, he and Mama talked. The Mayor of Albany had never been to our house before. I stood at the screen door and listened.

"The county commission and the city council have decided we want to honor your daughter Shirley," he began. "She has bought new recognition to both the town of Albany and Hawkins Valley, and we want to

The Angel Years

honor her for her contribution to the community."

"How are you going to do that?"

"We want to have a Shirley Temple Johnson Day celebration. We'll have a big parade, a public ceremony in the town square, and a banquet with speeches and flowers and such."

"Has all of this already been set up?"

"No. We didn't want to plan anything until we were sure your daughter could be present for the celebration. If we can get a commitment from your daughter for a given day, then we'll proceed."

"What day did you have in mind?"

"This upcoming August 30. That's five weeks away."

"Shirley is in Montana right now making a movie. I can call her and see if that date fits her schedule."

"That will be fine," he said. "I'll wait to hear from you."

***

On Sunday, Mama called Shirley and explained what the mayor had said.

"The director says this film will be finished sometime in July. After that, I'll have some free time. What day did you say?"

"August 30. It's a Saturday."

"Let me check the calendar."

A pause.

"I can do that. I'll have a month of free time and I can be there for the big celebration. And I'll be able to spend some time with my family."

Mama let out a whoop of joy.

"We can't wait to see you."

"And I can't wait to see my family."

"I love you, baby," Mama said.

"I love you too, Mama."

"Hallelujah!" Mama said as she hung up the phone. "Our baby is coming home!"

The Angel Years

8

When Shirley's new sedan rolled into our yard that afternoon on July 28, 1975, it was a day to remember. When she got out, she hugged Mama first, then me, and then Daddy. Audrey didn't hug her; she greeted Shirley with a cold "Hello."

Now, five years later, Shirley looked different. There was more maturity to her face, a little more sadness in her eyes, her hair and dress were more stylish, and she had put on a little weight, but, when she smiled, the sparkle in those deep blue eyes was just as bright as ever. The beautiful flower living inside her had not been touched by age.

"Oh, I'm so glad to be home again," she said. "Mama, can I sleep in Cornelia's room?"

"I knew that's what you would want. I've already made a bed in there for you."

***

For dinner that night, Mama cooked a meal of baked ham, green beans, mashed potatoes, and cornbread with blackberry cobbler. While we were eating, Shirley said she had some announcements to make after dinner. Once we were finished, however, Daddy and Audrey got up from the table and went into the living room. Daddy wanted to read the newspaper and Audrey wanted to listen to the Grand Ole Opry on the radio. After clearing off the table, Mama saw that Daddy and Audrey were absent, so she went into the living room to get them.

"What are y'all doing in here? Y'all come on back to the kitchen table. Shirley has got some things she wants to say."

"What do you want me for?" Daddy said. "I've told you a hundred times I don't know nothing about Hollywood stuff."

"What's the little princess going to do?" Audrey said. "Show us the little gold statue she won in Hollywood?"

"Y'all are part of this family and you need to hear what Shirley has to say."

Daddy looked up from the newspaper.

"Oh, all right," he said finally. "I guess it can't hurt nothing."

Daddy got up and started to the kitchen table.

Audrey had her ear glued to the radio.

"Audrey, come on in here and listen to what Shirley has to say."

The Angel Years

"I don't want to miss the Grand Ole Opry."

Anger flashed across Mama's face.

She walked across the room and turned off the radio.

"What did you do that for?"

"Because you're going to go to the kitchen table for this family meeting," she said, grabbing Audrey's arm and pulling her to her feet.

"All right! All right! Let go my arm!"

Once everyone was seated around the table, Shirley took the floor.

"First of all, I wanted to say I've missed y'all. Over the past five years, I've had great success in my career and now I want to do some things for my family."

Daddy's face formed a scowl. He and Audrey looked at one another with suspicion.

"What you going to do?" Daddy said.

"First of all, I'm going to pay off the farm and get you a new pickup."

An expression of pure shock flashed across Daddy's face. He pushed his glasses up on his nose so he could see Shirley better.

"I don't think I heard right. You said you're going to pay off the farm and buy me a new pickup?"

"That's right!"

"Not really?"

"Yes. Really."

Daddy was still in shock.

"You mean, after all these years, I'm going to be free of the mortgage on this farm?"

"That's right. Troy talked to the bank last week about the pay-off and the check has been sent. Troy said for you to go to the Ford dealership in Valdosta, pick out the truck you want, and call him. He'll send them a check."

"Well, hallelujah. My day has finally come. Thank you, Shirley. You have taken a big load off my mind."

Then he got up, went around the table, and hugged Shirley.

"Thank you!" he said again.

"You're welcome, Daddy."

"The little princess got rich in Hollywood and now she's showing off," Audrey said.

Shirley looked at Audrey but didn't reply

"What else you going to do, baby?" Mama said.

"Next I want to do something for Audrey."

Audrey's face screwed up in a scowl.

"What you going to do?"

"I'm going to pay for your operation. I told you years ago I would do it and now the day has come."

For a moment, Audrey looked at Shirley, then she looked at Daddy.

"You really going to pay for my operation?"

"Yes. I've contacted the hospital in Minnesota. Sophia will call you tomorrow and arrange to buy you a train ticket. You're going to be gone a week. Troy will send a check as soon as you check in to the hospital."

I could see the confusion in Audrey's eyes. Suddenly, she bowed her head on the table and started

The Angel Years

crying. Then, head down. she quickly got up from the table and rushed out of the room.

"She has made fun of and mocked you for so long," Mama said. "She doesn't know how to accept your kindness."

"That's all right, Mama."

Then Shirley reached down to the purse beside her chair and withdrew an envelope.

"Cornelia told me about the time you pawned your mother's brooch so I could have nice clothes and shoes to wear in junior high. Now I want to pay you back."

Mama's eyes widened with interest as Shirley opened the envelope.

"Here is five hundred dollars cash. I want you to go to Valdosta and buy ten new dresses for yourself and spend the rest of the money to buy anything you like."

Mama looked at the five hundred-dollar bills.

"Why would I want to buy ten dresses? I don't need ten dresses."

"Then spend the money however you like. I've been making lots of money and I want to spend it on the people I love."

***

On Monday of the following week, Audrey left for Minnesota to get her operation. On Tuesday, Daddy went into Albany and got the pay-off papers from the bank and, the following afternoon, he drove his new

Ford pickup into the front yard.

"Ila!" he called when he got out of the truck.

Mama came to the door.

"Come out here and look at my new truck."

"Looks like a nice one."

"It's about time I started enjoying life a little."

Over the next few weeks, I had never seen Daddy so happy. Somehow, Shirley's gifts gave him a whole new outlook on life. Suddenly, he started taking more pride in the farm. He had the barn roof painted. He hauled away two old broken-down pieces of sawmill machinery that had been rusting in the pasture for God knows how many years. He cleaned out the barn like he had been promising for years. He planted five fruit trees, two apple and three peach, along one side of the vegetable garden. He even talked about selling the mules and buying a tractor. I can honestly say that I had never seen my daddy so happy.

***

Audrey was gone eight days and, when she got back, it was really strange to see her without glasses. Now, at age 40 and without glasses, she became a totally new person. Everything about her, I mean absolutely everything, changed once she had the operation. Most of all, she now had confidence in herself; she wanted to be around other people, she laughed a lot more and, most of all, she started wearing lipstick and makeup.

The Angel Years

Only a week after she had the operation, she met Hollis Abernathy at a church social. Hollis wasn't much to look at, but he was good-natured, hard-working, and owned a trucking company over in Tifton. Anyway, over the next two weeks, Audrey and Hollis started dating. At the end of the second week, she was spending nights with him.

On Monday of the following week, Audrey returned to the family home.

Me, Mama, and Shirley were in the sitting room looking at old family photos. When Audrey came in the door, Mama glared at her.

"Where you been the last three nights?"

"I've been with Hollis."

"If you and him want to spend nights together, why don't y'all get married? It don't look good for you to go spending the night with a man, then coming back home when you get hungry."

Audrey turned angrily to Mama.

"I'm sick and tired of taking orders from you."

"If you come to this house and put your feet under my table, you'll take orders from me. This is my house."

"You go to hell!" Audrey said.

"You don't talk to me like that!"

The mother and daughter squared off as if they were about to fight.

"Wait!" Shirley shouted.

Quickly, she stepped between them.

"Please! Please! Let's have some peace. I've only

got another two weeks to spend with y'all and I want to enjoy your company and not listen to arguing and fighting."

Audrey looked at her mother then angrily stormed out of the room.

***

August 30, 1975, the day the Mayor of Albany designated for Shirley Temple Johnson day, was probably the happiest day of Mama's life. She got up early that morning, cooked breakfast, then took a bath and put on one of her new dresses. She checked herself several times in the mirror before we left. She had prepared a speech for the ceremony in the town square and she had Shirley read it and approve it. When Mama asked Audrey if she wanted to be in the parade, she said no. She and Hollis were going to Valdosta to look at wedding rings. Mama knew better than to ask Daddy to be in the parade. He had no time for social events.

So, on the morning of the big day, Shirley, Mama, and me loaded up in a big, black open-air car and, along with the Albany mayor and the Hawkins Valley county commissioner, we went riding down Main Street waving to the cheering crowds. There were marching bands, the local boy scouts, floats from the PTA, the Kiwanis Club, the National Guard, the Chamber of Commerce, and a whole bunch of other civic organizations I never heard of. At the ceremony, Mama

The Angel Years

gave her speech about being the mother of a celebrity. She was a little nervous at first, but once she got started, she calmed down and, once finished, received a rousing round of applause from the crowd. Next there were speeches by local politicians, well-wishes from old friends and, at the conclusion, the mayor presented Shirley with a key to the city. After the ceremony, Shirley spent over an hour signing autographs and greeting old friends and classmates. The following night, which was a Sunday, Mama delivered a speech to the Friends of the Hawkins Valley Library. This time, she looked like a professional speaker up there on the podium. A reporter with the *Albany Herald* and a TV crew from Atlanta were also in attendance and interviewed Mama. I took my camera and I snapped lots of pictures.

***

On Monday morning, I went to the Crossroads to get all of the photos I had made on Shirley Temple Johnson day. There were photos of the parade, a group photo of Mama, me, and Shirley, various shots of the Shirley signing autographs, and a picture of Mama speaking at the ceremony.

Shirley and I sat at the kitchen table and watched Mama open the package of photos and thumb through them. When she got to the photo of herself on the podium, all decked out in her new store-bought dress and speaking to the crowd, she lingered for a long moment, beaming from ear to ear with pride. Then she suddenly broke down in heart-rending sobs.

"Mama! Mama!!" I said. "What's wrong? I thought you would be happy to see the pictures."

"Oh, Cornpone," she said, using her apron to wipe away the tears. "I am so very, very happy. When I was a little girl growing up, I wanted to be somebody. I didn't want to be known all over Georgia, but I did want people in Hawkins Valley to know who I was. Now, thanks to Shirley, my dream has come true."

I went to comfort her.

"I guess I'm just getting old," she said as I hugged her. "As you get older, you see the fullness of your life. You know the ending is closer than the beginning."

Mama turned to Shirley and took her in her arms.

"Oh, baby," Mama said. "You've made me so happy. I love you."

"I love you too, Mama."

***

The following afternoon, I was so happy to be back at the pond painting birds and being alone with Shirley. I set up my easel in front of the old log and, while I sketched out and started painting a red cardinal, she lazed quietly on the old quilt reading a book about Alexander the Great. The only sounds were the twittering of the birds and the occasional splash of a

The Angel Years

catfish. Finally, she looked up from the book. She was in reflective mood.

"You know, in some ways, my life is like Alexander the Great's."

"How do you mean?"

"Like him, I don't have any more worlds to conquer. I am famous around the globe; I am rich and can buy anything I like; I have found the great love of my life in Rock… All of my dreams have come true."

"You sound like you're sad about your accomplishments."

"No. Not sad… just tired with the world."

"You've got to go on living," I said as I painted in the jet-black color in the cardinal's beak.

"Not necessarily. The bird of time has not far to fly. Death can be a beautiful thing."

I turned from my painting to look at her.

"Do you know what you're saying?"

"I know exactly what I'm saying."

"Aren't you afraid to die?"

"Death is a beginning, not an end."

My eyes filled with tears at the thought of losing her.

"Can I tell you a secret?"

"You can tell me anything."

"I've lived many lives. This life here with you and Mama is just one more. Just a different time. A different place. A different world."

"How do you know that?"

"I just know it!!"

"So what are your plans?"

"I'll be back in New York on Monday and meet Rock. We'll spend the night at the Rockefeller Plaza, then me and Troy will meet with the producer and sign the contracts for the war film the studio wants to make in Italy."

"What's the title of the war movie?"

"*Road to Glory*. It's the story of an American bomber pilot who falls in love with a member of the Italian resistance after they join forces to destroy a German ammunition depot near Palermo, Italy."

I looked up from my painting.

"Oh, I envy you so. I would love to see Italy. Florence. Venice. The Sistine chapel."

"I don't get a chance to do much sight-seeing."

"Yes, but just being there must be an incredible experience."

We were quiet for a moment.

"What are your plans after you finish the war movie?"

"Rock and I will go to Greece, probably Santorini, get married, and buy a white house with a blue roof overlooking the Aegean."

"Then what?"

"We'll live happily ever after."

A long silence.

Suddenly, Shirley burst out laughing.

"Why are you laughing?"

"Happily ever after… What a concept!"

The Angel Years

We were quiet for several minutes, then Shirley got up from the quilt to examine my painting of the cardinal.

"Oh, Cornelia, it's such a beautiful painting. I just love the scarlet red in the wings and the way the wing feathers graduate down to the lighter colors. You are so talented!"

"Thanks!"

"You know you could make money with your paintings, but you've got to get them into the hands of the right people."

"You mean people would pay me for my paintings?"

"Sure! You're good! Magazine and book publishers are always looking for talented artists."

"I never dreamed I could get paid for my painting. I always did it just for fun."

"When I leave, I want to take some of your work and show it to a friend of Troy's in Atlanta. Can you get me your five best paintings?"

***

An hour later, I had finished my painting. I folded up the easel and Shirley and I started back up the path to the house. When we reached the barn hallway, we could hear the loud voices of Mama and Audrey arguing at the clothesline.

"Don't hand me a clothespin until I'm ready," Mama was saying.

"You have to tell me when you're ready. I'm not a

mind reader."

A pause.

"Are you ready now?" Audrey asked.

"No!" Mama shouted. "Can't you see that I'm not ready? Don't you have eyes in your head?"

We listened for a moment, then Shirley turned to me.

"There's one more thing I need to do before I leave."

"What's that?"

"I'm going to stop this constant bickering between Mama and Audrey."

I peered at her.

"How in the world are you going to do that? That would take a miracle."

"Come on!"

As Shirley and I approached Mama and Shirley, two lines of hanging clothes in front of them shielded us from their view. Neither of them knew we were nearby. Then I watched as Shirley carefully slipped behind the nearest line of clothes. For a moment, she waited, then, just like she did with Truman, she raised her hands over her head with index fingers fully extended. She waited another moment, then suddenly, she stepped from behind the line of clothes and directed her index fingers toward Mama and Audrey. Instantly, lines of bright light emanated from her fingertips and enveloped the bodies of both Mama and Audrey. Instantly, both were frozen in space like statues in a public park. Audrey was posed handing a clothespin to Mama and Mama was

The Angel Years

reaching out her hand to take it.

I stared at the frozen forms of Mama and Audrey.

"Oh, my God!"

Shirley looked at me with an impish grin.

"Maybe I should leave them like this."

"Oh, you wouldn't do that?"

"No. I wouldn't."

Then, as if she knew exactly what she was doing, she held out her right hand and blew her breath on the palm. Suddenly, a small pile of glowing dust formed in the palm of the right hand. Then, using her left hand, she took a pinch and went to the motionless form of Audrey. Starting at the top of Audrey's head, she began sprinkling the dust in a downward spiral from the top of her head to her feet. Once finished with Audrey, she took another pinch of the dust and performed the same action on Mama. Now their motionless bodies were glowing from top to bottom with an indescribable brightness. I held my hand over my face to shield my eyes from the blinding light.

For a moment, Shirley stood back from her creation. Then, suddenly, she spoke.

"Never ever again will these two have another cross word with one another!"

The bodies of Mama and Audrey, glowing with a blindingly bright light, remained frozen in time and space.

"That should do it."

Then she stepped back and snapped her fingers.

Instantly, the bright illumination around their bodies disappeared and Mama and Audrey were back in motion.

"Mother, dear," Audrey said. "I have a clothespin for you."

Mama took the clothespin.

"Thank you, Audrey. I'll tell you when I'm ready for another."

Shirley and I burst out laughing like a couple of school girls.

Mama looked at us.

"Shirley, why are you and Cornpone laughing?" Mama said as she secured one of Daddy's old work shirts on the clothesline.

"Oh, it's nothing, Mama."

Mama accepted that, then turned back to Audrey.

"Audrey, dear, can you please hand me another clothespin?"

***

That night, Mama prepared a dinner of baked ham, turnip greens, mashed potatoes, and cornbread. Once we were all seated, Mama asked Daddy to bless the food. Once the prayer was said, the family was ready to eat.

"Audrey, dear," Mama said. "Can you please pass me the cornbread?"

"Sure," Audrey replied, reaching for the plate of cornbread.

The Angel Years

Mama took the plate.

"Would you also like some butter for your cornbread?" Audrey asked.

"Yes, please!"

Audrey reached for the butter dish and passed it to Mama.

"Thank you," Mama said.

"You're welcome," Audrey replied.

Daddy stopped serving his plate and peered first at Mama, then at Audrey.

"Why are you two being so all-fired nice to each other all of a sudden?"

"What are you talking about?" Mama said.

"You two are always fussing and jawing. I've never seen y'all be nice to one another. Did something happen?"

"No, nothing at all," Mama said.

"Nothing I know of," Audrey replied.

Shirley, sitting at the end of the table, winked at me. I winked back.

***

The following afternoon, we all gathered in the front yard of the family home to say good-bye to Shirley. I watched as she placed my paintings, along with her suitcases, in the back seat of the car.

She closed the rear door and turned to me.

"I'll show these to Troy's friend when I get back to

Atlanta."

Finally, each of us waited our turn to say goodbye. There was Mama, then Daddy, and finally me. Then Shirley looked to Audrey.

Suddenly, Audrey ran to Shirley and hugged her.

"Bye, Shirley! Thanks again for paying for my operation. Me and Hollis are getting married next month. I owe it all to you."

"You're welcome."

Inside my heart, I smiled. After all those years, my oldest sister had finally found the kindness in her heart.

Shirley started to get into the car.

"One last thing…" Mama said.

"What's that, Mama?"

"You've done something special for everybody in the family except Cornelia. Horace has a new pickup and the farm is paid off. Audrey got her operation and found Hollis, and I got the recognition I always wanted. What you going to do for Cornelia?"

I was embarrassed.

"Mama!" I said. "Shirley doesn't have to do anything for me. I love her whether she does anything for me or not."

Shirley smiled and looked at me.

"Her time will come."

The car engine started and we waved good-bye one last time, then watched as the big black sedan pulled out of the driveway and disappeared down the highway.

The Angel Years

9

The early morning of October 5, 1975 is a day I will always remember. I was in bed at the family home sound asleep, when I heard the phone ring. I woke up and looked at the clock. It was 3:30. I wondered who in the world could be calling at this hour. In the living room, I saw a light come on and could hear Mama answering the phone. Moments later, I had my clothes on and was in the living room.

Mama was already crying when I reached her. I knew something was wrong. Bad wrong.

"Mama! Who is it?"

She didn't hear me at first; she was hanging on to every word the caller was saying.

"Mama, who is it?"

Then, seeing my persistence, she wiped tears on the shoulder of her nightgown and removed the receiver.

"It's Troy."

"What is it?"

For a long moment, she looked at me, then burst into

sobs.

"Mama! Tell me what's wrong!"

"Cornpone..."

Then she stopped.

"Mama!" I shouted. "Tell me what's wrong!"

Then she blurted out the words.

"Shirley is dead!"

Suddenly, I felt my heart go into my mouth.

"Oh, no!" I said. "Not Shirley! Not our beloved Shirley!"

Then I ran back to my bedroom and collapsed on the bed in tears.

That afternoon, I got the details.

Earlier that night, Troy had received a phone call from the producer of the war film Shirley and Rock were making in Italy. While shooting an action sequence, the helicopter they were riding in crashed into a radio tower and all those aboard, including Shirley and Rock, were killed instantly. She was 21.

***

Four days later, Shirley's body was returned to Hawkins Valley. Our little community had never seen a funeral like that. The church house at Old Harmony wasn't big enough to hold all of the people and, during the services, there must have been two or three thousand people standing around outside. There were political bigwigs and television cameras and newspaper reporters

The Angel Years

from New York, Los Angeles, and London. It was the biggest funeral ever held in Hawkins Valley. We all just cried and cried.

***

A month after the funeral, Mama was still grieving. She said it was as if the good Lord had sent a miracle to our family to spread happiness and joy among us.

"God just let us borrow her for just a little while. He never meant for us to keep her very long…"

Then she bowed her head and began weeping softly into a handkerchief. Then I remembered what Shirley had said about living other lives. Somehow, in my heart, I knew she had just gone on to the next life. After that, somehow, I didn't feel as bad. During the entire time I had known her, she never once made mention of or asked who her real mother was. As far as she was concerned, Mama was her one and only mother. On the other hand, she had such a deep spiritual connection with the universe that I suspect she may have known, but she never mentioned it. She was too gracious to mention it.

Later that year, Mama and Daddy put up a headstone on her grave down at Old Harmony. It read:

Shirley Temple Johnson

1954 -1975

John Isaac Jones

"Heaven Couldn't Wait!"

***

So, just like that, the innocent little child who had changed all of our lives was gone. As it turned out, I didn't learn what Shirley did for me until the following spring. In March, some six months after the funeral, I got a call from a woman who was an assistant director at the Georgia Department of Wildlife in Atlanta. Her name was Francesca Romano. She said she loved the paintings Shirley had shown her the previous fall and asked if I would be interested in doing a book of illustrations for the department. The books would go into libraries, state museums, and bookstores, and be an official record of the state's birdlife. I told her I would be delighted.

Once the book was published, it was a big hit. It sold oodles and oodles of copies. Thanks to Shirley, the door to success had been opened, and not only was I making money with my paintings, but I was making more money than I could ever have imagined. Shirley had gotten me my big break.

But that's not all.

After the book had been out for about six months, I was having lunch in the cafeteria at the state capital with Francesca when she introduced me to her brother

The Angel Years

Vincent. He was forty-three, an electrical engineer, and had recently moved from New York to Atlanta to work for Georgia Power Company. He said Francesca had told him about me, he liked my book and, before we parted, he asked for a dinner date. That was the very last thing I had expected, but, when he asked, a little voice inside me told me to accept. And I did. Over the next two months, we dated, became close friends, and eventually were married. I was 37. Once we set up housekeeping in East Atlanta, Vincent said he wanted me to learn to cook Italian like his mother used to make when he was a child growing up in Brooklyn. His favorite dish was ravioli he said, an Italian delicacy made with tiny pieces of fresh meat inside squares of chewy pasta. The first time I set about preparing ravioli for my new husband, I remembered what Shirley had said ten years earlier while we were shelling purple hull peas.

***

So ends the story of this special little person that God or fate or destiny or something sent into our lives. For whatever reason, she appeared out of the blue and, over the span of some twenty years, changed all of our lives for the better. It was something none of us could ever have expected, much less predicted. Now, many years later, when I think back on it, it all seems so far, far away and so incredibly unreal. The whole thing was like an absolute miracle. Finally, for me, the most amazing part of the entire episode was this simple fact: if it hadn't been for Mama's single deciding vote, none of it would ever have happened.

The End

The Angel Years

Dear Reader:

Thanks for taking the time to read my novella *The Angel Years*.

If you enjoyed it, please consider telling your friends or posting a short review.

Reviews make a difference.

It only takes a few words and it can help enormously.

Without your reviews and favorable mentions, my hard work might go unnoticed.

Thanks a million for your support.

John I. Jones

John Isaac Jones

A * JIJ * Book
Copyright 2019 by John Isaac Jones

All rights reserved. No part of this book may be reproduced or transmitted in any form by any means, electronic or mechanical, including photocopying and recording, or by any information storing and retrieval system, except as may be expressly permitted by the 1976 Copyright Act or by the publisher. Requests for permission should be sent to johni@johnisaacjones.com
This book is a work of fiction and any resemblance to persons, living or dead, or places, events, and locales is purely coincidental. The characters are reproductions of the author's imagination and used fictitiously.
Manufactured in the United States of America
First edition/First printing

Editing and formatting by BZHercules.com
Cover art designed by Leilani Doombosch

www.ingramcontent.com/pod-product-compliance
Lightning Source LLC
Chambersburg PA
CBHW020657300426
44112CB00007B/423